Selected Issues in the EU-Korea Relations

This work was supported by the 2019 Hankuk University of Foreign Studies Research Fund

Selected Issues in the EU-Korea Relations

Bongchul Kim / Tomasz Wierzbowski
Hayann Lee / Ewa Motylińska

HU:iNE

Selected Issues in the EU-Korea Relations
by *Bongchul Kim, Tomasz Wierzbowski, Hayann Lee, Ewa Motylińska*

Cover design by HyeJin Cho
Design edited by EwhanD&B (+82-2-2254-4301)
Edited by Sunho Shin, HyeonJeong Park, and EwhanD&B
Printed by NEO printech (+82-2-718-3111)
Published in Republic of Korea by Huine, an imprint of Hankuk University of Foreign Studies University Knowledge Contents and Press, Seoul.
http://press.hufs.ac.kr
First printing, June 14, 2019
ISBN 979-11-5901-583-0 93360
Price 18,000 Won

Preface

Preface

Year 2018 marked 55 anniversary of the establishment of the diplomatic relations between the European Union (EU) and Korea. Over that time, both of the partners have become major global actors and they have intensified wide-ranging cooperation to meet the common challenges. Despite the geographical distance, the bilateral relations between current 28 EU Member States and Korea have flourished in every dimension; the EU is Korea's 3rd largest and Korea is the EU's 8th largest trading partner with annual trade in goods, with their overall trade volume reaching EUR 100 billion.

Today Korea is one of the EU's ten strategic partners, with bonds built on agreements from economics, politics, security cooperation, collaboration in areas of science, technology and culture. As the division remains within Korean Peninsula, the EU strives to play more significant role by furthering its relations with North Korea in shaping the future of regional integration in Northeast Asia.

The purpose of this book is to raise awareness of the role of the EU in Korea and promote EU-Korea relations as an exemplification of a successful collaboration. The authors in each chapter of this book examine the evolution of the EU-Korea relations and address selected aspects of bilateral ties that, requires further attention.

Chapter one examines the historical background and the origin of the EU-Korea relations and describes current status of bilateral ties in the field of economics, politics, culture as well as science and technology perspectives. Chapter two focuses on the laws on the cooperation between Korea and four Central and Eastern European countries where the Visegrád Group originated from. Chapter three analyses and compares the EU and Korea's policies on Small and Medium Size Enterprises and Start-ups. Final chapter examines the reconciliation processes in Europe and Northeast Asia based on two dyads; Korean-Japanese and German-Polish Relations after World War II.

Four authors of this book represent profound level of expertise in the EU and the Korean Peninsula. What makes them exceptional is that Korean authors completed their education in Europe and the European authors did so in Korea. This background has greatly contributed in making their perspectives uniquely insightful. The hope is this book will contribute to a deeper understanding of each partners and expand the areas of the cooperation.

The Authors

Contents

Selected Issues in the EU-Korea Relations

Chapter 1. European Union's Role in the Korean Peninsula: Reflecting on the Years of Relations

European Union's Role in the Korean Peninsula: Reflecting on 55 Years of Relations

Tomasz Wierzbowski

I. Introduction

The European Union (EU) is an unprecedented supranatural organization consisted of 28 Member States that have agreed to cooperate on various economic, political, and social matters. The predecessor of the EU was established after World War II in an effort to foster economic cooperation and thus interdependence between neighbouring countries, as a result they would be less prone to conflict. What began as an economic union, gradually has changed into comprehensive organization embracing various policy areas, from health, environment, climate change, migration, to security, justice and external relations.

Despite the partition of the peninsula and the Korean War that broke out in 1950 and ended in 1953 without a peace agreement, Korea has developed into one of Asia's most affluent countries. Korea being one of the biggest world's major economies would not be an understatement. In 2018, the EU and Korea celebrated 55th anniversary of establishing diplomatic relations. Over those 55 years, both the EU and Korea have become major global actors and at the same time they have intensified wide-ranging cooperation in order to meet the common challenges.

Today, Korea is one of the ten EU's strategic partners, with bonds built on agreements covering economic, political, and security cooperation, as well as, collaboration in areas of science, technology and innovation and culture exchange. As the Korean Peninsula has remained divided, the EU also maintain relationship with North Korea and could play more significant role in shaping the future of regional integration in Northeast Asia.

This chapter outlines the historical events that laid foundation to the current status of the EU's involvement in the Korean Peninsula examining the present economic, political, cultural and scientific cooperation between EU and Korea. In conclusion, the research takes a normative approach and argue how the EU could become more engaged in forging international community's policy towards the North Korean issues.

II. Historical Overview

1. Before the Establishment of Diplomatic Relations

Before 1498, when the Portuguese fleet of Vasco da Gama reached India's shore, the relationships between European states and Asia were essentially non-existent.[1] During the following 500 years the Korean Peninsula was treated rather exceptionally, when European powers executed their semi-imperial policies in Asia. Korea remained under influence of China and later Japan which forced modernization of Korea.[2] Korea liberalized from the Japanese occupation (1910-1945) in August 1945 with the end of World War II and was promptly divided into two separate political entities – North Korea (officially, the Democratic People's Republic of Korea above the 38 parallel of the Korean Peninsula and South Korea (officially the Republic of Korea) in the southern part of the Korean Peninsula.

According to Historian Bruce Cumings, there was no historical or internal justification for the division of Korean Peninsula, as it was a part of the global political game by the United States (US) and the Union of Soviet Socialist Republics (USSR), as Joseon - the political predecessor of later divided Koreas - was a single political and social entity and even under the Japanese occupa-

---

1) Nayan Chanda, "When Asia Was One," *Global Asia* 1, no. 1 (2006).
2) David C Kang, *East Asia before the West: Five Centuries of Trade and Tribute* (Columbia University Press, 2010).

tion Koreans inhabiting Korean Peninsula shared the same language, culture, history, national heritage, customs and habits. It is without doubt that any differences, whether social or political, developed as a result of the division of the Peninsula facilitated by ideological differences and broader regional as well as global politics.

The division of Korean Peninsula was soon followed by the indecisive Korean War (1950-1953) with 10 European countries actively participating in the Korean conflict under the US led United Nations (UN) coalition forces. Although the United Kingdom (UK) was second only to the US in the contribution it made to the UN effort in the Korean Peninsula with 87,000 British troops taking part in the Korean conflict, and over 1,000 British death soldiers, the European involvement was rather symbolic.[3]

After the Korean War, both South and North Korea had been receiving significant support from their allies. The European influence was highly limited except for the Neutral Nations Supervisory Commission (NNSC). Immediately after the War, four European countries: Czechoslovakia, Poland, Sweden and Switzerland were invited to form the NNSC - a supervising body that was supposed to carry out supervision and inspections in order to secure the implementation of the Korean Armistice

---

3) Gordon L Rottman, *Korean War Order of Battle: United States, United Nations, and Communist Ground, Naval, and Air Forces, 1950-1953* (Greenwood Publishing Group, 2002).

Agreement sub-paragraphs 13(c) and 13(d), which aimed at preventing reinforcements on the Korean Peninsula. The Inspection Teams from four European countries were completely dismantled in 1956[4] and the role of the NNSC was reduced when Czechoslovakian and Polish officers established a camp on the Northern side of Joint Security Area (JSA) in the Demilitarized Zone (DMZ) and their Swedish and Swiss counterparts became located on the Southern side of JSA. The role of the NNSC has changed over time; After the peaceful split of Czechoslovakia (1993). Both the Czech Republic and Slovakia agreed that the Czech Republic would take over its membership in the NNSC. The Czech members left their camp in JSA in 1993 and ever since, the Czech Republic has not taken part in NNSC meetings.

During the first half of the 1990s, North Korea repealed its invitation to participate in the NNSC also to Poland, claiming that the NNSC had completed its activities and, that due to political changes, Poland could not be considered a "neutral nation. Although this statement was not accepted to by the Polish government, permanent representatives to the NNSC that had been stationed in Panmunjom on the northern side of JSA were withdrawn from their camp under North Korea's pressure in February 1995.[5] However, Poland has officially remained a member of the NNSC and Polish officers join their Swiss and

---

4) Christian Birchmeier, Marceli Burdelski, and Eugeniusz Jendraszczak, *50-Lecie Komisji Nadzorczej Państw Neutralnych W Korei* (A. Marszałek, 2003).

5) Ibid.

Swedish counterparts and participate in the NNSC meetings twice a year.

Although the primary mission of the NNSC from the Armistice Agreement is to supervise, investigate and inspect five ports of entry to the Korean Peninsula (in both South and North) was practically cancelled in 1956, since 2010 the NNSC has been implementing the Expanded Tasks in the spirit of the Armistice Agreement through observation of the UN Command, Military Armistice Commission (UNCMAC) operations in the DMZ; education and orientation to relevant units and institutions; as well as observation of large US/South Korea and South Korea-only military exercises.

Western European countries engaged further in the regional integration and signed Treaty of Rome (1957), which created the European Economic Community (EEC), the European Atomic Energy Community (Euratom) and established a customs union. However, they remained politically absent in the Korean Peninsula where both Koreas were receiving significant support from their allies. The US provided Korea with more than USD 100 million annually with the total size of South Korean budget in 1951 coming to USD 120 million.[6]

During the early years following the armistice, Korea was almost entirely dependent on the US for food and consumer goods. The support involved not only direct money inflow, but

---

6) Bruce Cumings, *Korea's Place in the Sun : A Modern History*, Updated ed. (New York: W. W. Norton, 2005).

also security commitment, military equipment and technology transfer as well as significant cultural and people-to-people exchange. The direct financial aid terminated in the 1960s with a shift in the assistance model where the national development was achieved more through strengthening the economic interdependence and trade rather than direct financial contribution. It is estimated that between 1946 and 1978 the total amount of grants and loans offered by the US to Korea reached approximately USD 60 billion.[7]

Extensive Soviet and Chinese supports were vital factors of the development of North Korea and its reconstruction after the Korean War. The founding father of North Korea, Kim Il Sung played successful game between two communist rivals to maximize his own interest. Right after the War, he made all the debts being cancelled or postponed and he secured 1 billion rubbles-worth support in direct monetary aid as well as in the form of industrial and military equipment, consumer good and technology transfer.[8] The economic growth rate of North Korea was estimated to be the highest in the world, averaging 39% between 1953 and 1960.[9] The central planned economy started to reach its limits of output and major disparities caused problems

---

7) Guardian, "South Korea: A Model of Development?," *The Guardian* (2011), https://www.theguardian.com/global-development/poverty-matters/2011/nov/28/south-korea-development-model.

8) Charles K Armstrong, "The Destruction and Reconstruction of North Korea, 1950-1960," *The Asia-Pacific Journal* 8, no. 51 (2010).

9) Joseph Sang-hoon Chung, *The North Korean Economy: Structure and Development* (University Microfilms, 1966).

in systematic economic development. Especially, power supply sector - oil and electricity production lagged behind other industrial sectors.

To address these problems North Korean authorities once again leaned towards its social allies with request for aid. The Sino-Soviet relations worsened resulting both leaders of China and the USSR competed for leadership in the communist world.[10] Once again Kim Il-sung successfully manipulated international situation and ideological dispute between two superpowers and secured aid for North Korea that continued to flow from China and the USSR despite significant differences between the two. As a result, in 1960s North Korea was cancelled USD 190 million debt in military loans and allowed for further USD 35 million of economic aid from the Soviets.[11] By playing political games between Moscow and Beijing, Pyongyang also managed to secure USD 105 million in long-term loans in the first half of 1960s.[12]

In terms of total economic output the South became stronger than the North in 1965[13], while GDP per capita indicator for

---

10) Danhui Li and Yafeng Xia, "Competing for Leadership: Split or Détente in the Sino-Soviet Bloc, 1959–1961," *The International History Review* 30, no. 3 (2008).

11) Zhihua Shen and Yafeng Xia, "China and the Post-War Reconstruction of North Korea, 1953-1961," *North Korea International Documentation Project Working Paper* 4 (2012).

12) Ibid.

13) Robert Daniel Wallace, *North Korea and the Science of Provocation : Fifty Years of Conflict-Making* (Jefferson, North Carolina: McFarland & Company, Inc., Publishers, 2016).

both Koreas was said to reach the same level around 1973.[14] According to the UN statistics,[15] (South) Korean GDP per capita surpassed that of North Korea for the first time in 1974 valuing USD 571 against USD 515. The difference increased to almost three times by 1980 with (South) Korean GDP per capita equalling USD 1,735 and North Korean – USD 639.

2. Recent Relations

With the end of the Cold War, since 1990s, the overall political landscape for the EU and the Korean Peninsula started to change. By the mid-1990s North Korean economy exposed all its inherent weaknesses of central-planned economy alongside with vulnerability to external political relations. North Korea's failing economic policies, demise of the USSR, collapse of the energy supply for production sector together with unfortunate weather conditions lead to almost total failure of the economy[16] which was followed by the inability of the state to feed its citi-

14) Daniel Tudor and James Pearson, *North Korea Confidential : Private Markets, Fashion Trends, Prison Camps, Dissenters and Defectors* (Tokyo ; Rutland, Vermont ; Singapore: Tuttle Publishing, 2015).

15) National Accounts Main Aggregates Database: https://unstats.un.org/unsd/snaama/resQuery.asp, (accessed: January 12, 2018). The credibility of this data is questionable as there is no explanation how the UN estimated the value of North Korean GDP. Some researchers claim that data are provided by the North Korean authorities.

16) Meredith Woo-Cumings, "The Political Ecology of Famine: The North Korean Catastrophe and Its Lessons," (ADBI Research Paper Series, 2002).

zens.

On the contrary, since 1960s, the Korean economy grew at an average annual rate of nearly 9%, and per capita income increased more than a hundredfold. By mid-90s Korea together with Hong Kong, Singapore and Taiwan, became one of the leading Asia's 'tiger economies'. This economic boom of East Asian countries created new opportunities and demands for international and intercontinental trade which contributed to the rationale for the establishment of the Asia-Europe Meeting (ASEM) in 1996.[17] Ever since ASEM has remained a platform for dialogue aimed to foster political, economic and socio-cultural cooperation between the members.[18]

The real significance of ASEM has been disputed[19] - Asian states remained suspicious of each other in terms of substantial regional integration, which jammed further inter-regional collaboration[20] and ASEM has not significantly stimulated much in the way of deeper cooperation and integration.[21] Further-

---

17) Michael K Connors, Rémy Davison, and Jörn Dosch, *The New Global Politics of the Asia Pacific* (Routledge, 2011).

18) Lay Hwee Yeo, *Asia and Europe: The Development and Different Dimensions of Asem* (Routledge, 2004).

19) Michael Reiterer, "Asia-Europe Meeting (Asem): Fostering a Multipolar World Order through Inter-Regional Cooperation," *Asia Europe Journal* 7, no. 1 (2009).

20) David Shambaugh and Michael Yahuda, *International Relations of Asia* (Rowman & Littlefield, 2014).

21) Wilhelm Hofmeister and Yeo Lay Hwee, "The Asia-Europe Meeting: Engagement, Enlargement and Expectations," *Singapore: EU Centre and Konrad-Adenauer-Stiftung* (2010).

more, this apathy of ASEM[22] illustrates the differentiation in values between the EU and Asian countries. General European preferences in values focused on deepening regional integration, multilateralism, soft power and inter-regional foreign policy are not equally shared by Asian states, including Korea.[23]

Due to these ideological and political constrains the relationships between the EU and Korea focused particularly on economic cooperation. Since the problematic Doha Development Agenda (DDA) Round under the World Trade Organization (WTO) both the EU and Korea turned into bilateral dialogues with other countries. The negotiations for the EU–Korea Free Trade Agreement (FTA) started in 2006; the agreement was signed in October 2009 and came into force provisionally after ratification by both legislatures on 1 July 2011.[24] The EU-Korea FTA, the first EU's trade deal with an Asian country, was an aftermath of the establishment of the EU-Korea 'Strategic Partnership' in 2009 and 'Framework Agreement' in 2010.

22) Sebastian Bersick, "Yeo Lay Hwee/Wilhelm Hofmeister (Eds.), the Asia–Europe Meeting. Engagement, Enlargement and Expectations (Eu Centre in Singapore: 2010), 113 Pages," (Springer, 2010).
23) Ibid.
24) Formal ratification of the FTA was concluded in December 2015.

III. The EU-Korea Cooperation

1. The Economic Cooperation

The emergence of the economic and trade cooperation is rooted in a long history of diplomatic relations between the EU and Korea originated in 1965.[25] In the 1990s cooperation between the EU and Korea reached a new level with a rapid increase in trade exchanges. In 1996, the EU and Korea signed a Framework for Trade and Cooperation (ratified in 2001) and a Joint Declaration on Political Dialogue. These two documents paved the way for establishment of a formal system for regular economic and political cooperation. In the following year, the EU joined an executive board of the Korean Peninsula Energy Development Organization (KEDO). The new millennium has been marked by further strengthening of economic relationship between the EU and Korea.[26]

The development of the EU economy in terms of employment and growth is basically sustained by export. The EU Member States, being aware of the benefits that come from external trade, have authorized the European Commission to negotiate FTAs with Asian partners. India, Korea and the Association of Southeast Asian Nations (ASEAN) were set as priorities.

---

25) Cumings, *Korea's Place in the Sun : A Modern History*.
26) Axel Marx et al., "Eu–Korea Relations in a Changing World Project: Main Results and Recommendations," *Asia Europe Journal* 12, no. 3 (2014).

Korea was the fourth largest economy in Asia and the 11th largest in the world with a GDP of over USD 1,531 billion (2017). Therefore, in recent years, Korea became one of the strategic economic partners of the EU. Korea was the ninth largest export destination for goods coming from the EU's countries whereas the EU was Korea's third major export market in 2018.[27]

The nature of trade between the EU and Korea is perfectly in line with current global trends, with focus on technology-intensive sectors, such as telecommunication equipment, machinery and transport equipment, and chemicals. Annual bilateral trade in goods is worth approximately EUR 100 billion and imports and exports are well balanced (Eurostat, 2018). Trade between the EU and Korea has grown steadily since 2010 (16% in 2017). Since the FTA entered into force, the EU's exports to Korea increased by a year-on-year growth of over 9% whereas imports from Korea into the EU have also increased, but not by as much (6%) and, as a result, from 2013 until 2016 the EU's long-held trade deficit with Korea turned into a surplus. In 2017, Korea obtained again a trade surplus of EUR 2 million, due to a substantial increase of exports (20%), in context marked by the economic recovery in the EU.

As of 2015, Korea was the EU's 12th largest trading partner in services. Exchange in services between the EU and Korea has intensively increased over the last few years. Nevertheless, total

---

27) Statistical Office of the European Communities. *EUROSTAT: Regional statistics.: Reference guide*. Luxembourg: Eurostat. (2018)

Trade in goods between EU and Korea, 2015-2017, billion EUR

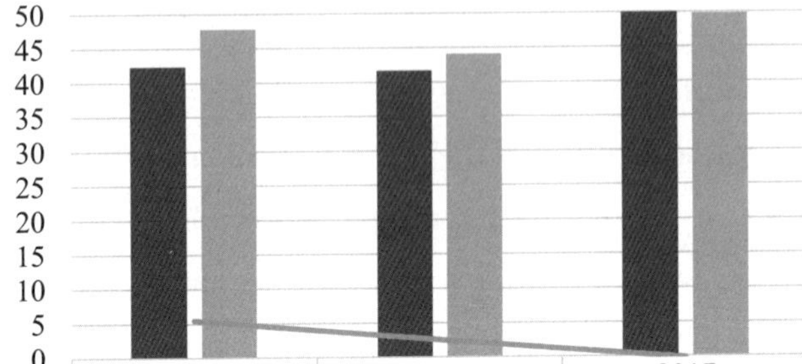

	2015	2016	2017
EU Imports	42.4	41.7	50
EU Exports	47.8	44.1	49.8
Balance	5.4	2.5	-0.2

trade of services between them represents only about 1.1% of the EU's total trade in services, which indicates some unexploited potential. Trade in services between the partners has gradually increased by 47% in the period 2010-2015. During the time EU's export of services to Korea grew significantly by 46% to EUR 11 billion whereas Korean export increased by 323%. The EU's exports to Korea are concentrated in a few sectors, in particular: business services (280%), transport (17%), and travel.

Foreign Direct Investment (FDI) stock is a reliable indicator of the strength of the economic relationship between the parties. While financial flows fluctuate, the data on stock reflect investors' long-term commitment. According to Eurostat, the EU FDI to Korea increased from 2014 to 2015 by 8% to reach EUR 49.7 billion, accounting for over 20% of the FDI stock in Korea. In 2016 the EU's FDI stock in Korea reached EUR 50 billion, which was 12% more than in 2015. Overall, in the following years the

Trade in Services between EU and Korea, 2015-2017, billion EUR

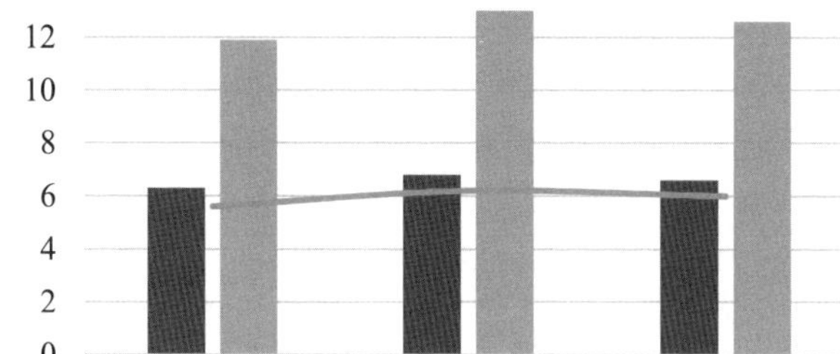

	2015	2016	2017
EU Imports	6.3	6.8	6.6
EU Exports	11.9	13.1	12.6
Balance	5.6	6.2	6

EU Imports EU Exports Balance

FDI from the EU into Korea grew by a 140% from 2010 to EUR 5.5 billion in 2017. The EU, with 32% of total FDI stock in Korea, is by far the largest source of FDI in Korea ahead of Japan (26%) and the US (19%). On the opposite side, Korean investments in the EU countries increased by approximately 19% in the same period.[28]

In order to enhance trade and investment exchanges, two parties began negotiating for the EU-Korea FTA in 2007 and officially signed the FTA in 2010 in Brussels. The FTA has been conditionally applied since July 2011 and came officially into force in December 2015. This first FTA of EU with an Asian country was a significant step forward in economic relations between the two parties. Furthermore, the EU-Korea FTA is claimed to be the most comprehensive and ambitious trade

28) Statistical Office of the European Communities. *EUROSTAT: Regional statistics.: Reference guide*. Luxembourg: Eurostat. (2018)

Foreign direct investment 2016, billion EUR

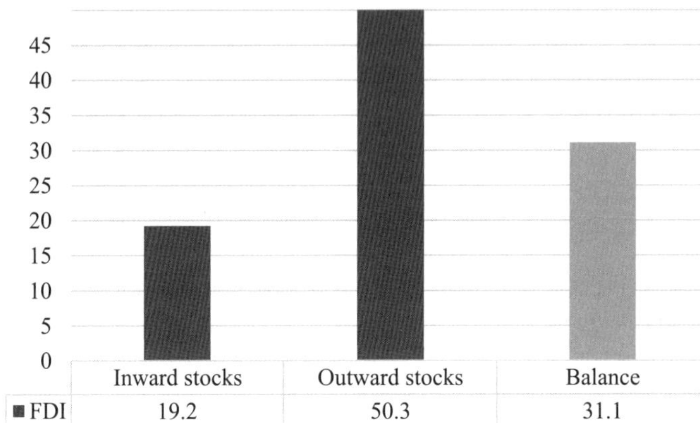

agreement signed by the EU. The FTA not only eliminates almost 99% of duties on both sides within five years from signing it but also deals with non-tariff barriers. The FTA gradually eliminates tariffs for industrial and agricultural goods, thus only a very limited number of mainly agricultural goods is excluded from tariff elimination. Moreover, the FTA includes provisions concerning competition policy, intellectual property rights, transparency in regulation, government procurements and sustainable development.[29]

The FTA is put into practice through an annual Trade Committee and an Intellectual Property Dialogue. Additionally, in order to monitor implementation of the FTA, seven specialized committees and seven working groups have been established.

---

29) https://publications.europa.eu/en/publication-detail/-/publication/4878c0b2-58be-4db9-8984-8982c8fb84b1 (retrieved March 10, 2019)

While annual Trade Committee at ministerial level is a supervisory body created to ensure correct operation of the Agreement, specialized committees and working groups provide a space for addressing concerns of engaged parties and to seek for closer regulatory cooperation. The Committee addressed particularly issues related to sustainable development and labour rights. Also, the European side pushed for further progress in European beef export to Korea, and the protection of intellectual property rights. The Committee also raised the topic of possible amendments to the FTA, to make it work more effectively for both sides.[30]

Alongside with the ongoing meetings at working- and higher level between the EU and Korean administration, specialized formal committees and working groups also meet at least once a year and discuss non-tariff barriers across all sectors including the automotive, pharmaceuticals, cosmetics, medical devices and electronics sectors. The objective of these committees is to practically carry out continuous regulatory dialogue (in particular for non-tariff commitments, services and regulatory convergence).

Despite these mechanisms, some implementation and bilateral trade issues remain problematic with persisting issues in the automotive, food and pharmaceutical areas. In the food sector, complicated authorization procedures still affect EU agricul-

30) https://eeas.europa.eu/delegations/south-korea_ko/38576/7th%20meeting%20of%20the%20Trade%20Committee%20of%20the%20EU-Korea%20Free%20Trade%20Agreement%20(FTA) (retrieved March 10, 2019)

tural exports, in particular for EU beef and pork exports. Implementation is still pending in the area of intellectual property rights, especially in the area of public performance rights and geographical indications. Furthermore, there is no provision in the EU-Korea FTA which would exempt repaired goods from customs duties on re-entry to Korea or EU after repair in the EU or Korea.[31] Korea has not yet fully implemented the "Trade and Sustainable Development" chapter of the FTA regarding labour rights. The EU is increasingly concentrating on the broader implications of trade to reflect EU societal and political concerns.

Nonetheless, the FTA has provided an outstanding result. Owing to trade liberalization the EU-Korea trade flows increased considerably, boosting competitiveness of companies and providing a wider, cheaper choice to consumers both in Europe and in Korea. In general, the FTA has contributed ultimately to improving the livelihood of citizens, creating jobs, increasing wealth in both parties and has deepened the strategic partnership between the partners.

1. Science, Technology and Innovation and Education Cooperation

Being aware that Science, Technology and Innovation play a crucial role in shaping the world economy, the EU and Korea

31) https://korea.ahk.de/fileadmin/AHK_Korea/Navigation_menu/KORUM/KORUM_75.pdf (retrieved: March 10, 2019)

signed the Agreement on the Scientific and Technological Cooperation in 2007. What is more, the Agreement for Cooperation between Euratom and Korea in the field of fusion energy research has been in force since 2006 and the EU-Korea Joint Science & Technology Cooperation Committee (JSTCC) has been held biennially. The work of JSTCC focuses mainly on five research areas: ICT, nanotechnology, health, energy and satellite navigation.

The research and innovation support program Horizon 2020 running 2014-2020, brings together researchers and industries within and outside of Europe, enabling them to obtain and exchange knowledge and expertise in the respective fields of science and technology. Horizon 2020 facilitates contact with specialists all over the world, as well as the creation of extensive networks between interested parties. During 2014-2015 under Horizon 2020, Korean applicants submitted 61 proposals, involving 71 participations in collaborative actions, leading to 10 successful projects, involving 13 participations, with a success rate of 21.3% (as compared to 10.6% overall). Due to overall success of Horizon 2020, the European Commission decided to launch the new research and innovation program from 2021 to 2027, 'Horizon Europe' where more international cooperation for science, technology and innovation is expected to take place world widely.

The EU and Korea are strongly aware of gains that expanded academic links may bring. The leading role of Korea in research and technological development, makes it a highly valued partner. Hence, they signed the Joint Declaration that provide the framework for a policy dialogue on issues related to higher education in 2013. The first policy dialogue was held in Brussels in 2016 to discuss practical ways of strengthening collaboration in higher education and to expand an exchange of best practice, policy review, and knowledge building. They through programs like Erasmus+ and Industrialized Countries Instrument - Education Cooperation Program (ICI-ECP) managed to develop joint degrees, partnerships and mobility programs which have enhanced academic exchanges and prepared students for the increasingly globalized and competitive labour market.

Furthermore, four Korean Universities (Hankuk University of Foreign Studies; Seoul National University; Yonsei University; Pusan National University) became hosts for Jean Monnet Centres of Excellence, which act as focal points of competence and knowledge on EU-related subjects. Additionally, there is one EU Centre at the Korea University. Other initiatives created to strengthen cooperation in higher education include Erasmus Mundus Joint Master' s Degrees (EMJMD); Research Fellowship Program - Marie Skłodowska-Curie Actions; Jean-Monnet Programs for teaching and research in the field of European studies; International Credit Mobility (Student mobility between Program and non-EU countries) and Joint Doctoral Programs.

In May 2018, EURAXESS - Researchers in Motion initiative was launched in Korea. This is a European Commission initiative delivering information and support services to professional researchers. Backed by the EU, Member States and associated countries, it supports researcher mobility and career development, while enhancing scientific collaboration between Europe and Korea.

Another initiative created in order to advance and promote the cooperation between the EU and non-EU countries in the field of science and technology is the EU Partnership Instrument (PI). As a direct result of the collaboration between the EU Delegations to Korea and its public authorities, companies, civil society organizations, universities and individuals, a number of PI projects have emerged in the country. The key PI projects covers various topics such as environment and green economy (The EU Gateway Program); climate change (Implementation of an Emissions Trading System in Korea); trade facilitation (Implementation of ILO Fundamental Convention 111 in Korea and the EU Member States).

The both partners recognize the importance of educating highly skilled workforce to deal with challenges of globalized world. They also recognize the crucial contribution higher education makes to developing a globally competitive, knowledge-based economy and so boosting growth and jobs inter alia through the promotion of entrepreneurship.

2. Cultural Cooperation

Recognizing the crucial role of culture in international relations, the EU adopted a 'Strategy for International Cultural Relations' in 2016. The aim of the Strategy is to encourage cultural exchange between the EU and its partners in different parts of the world, as well as, to promote freedom of expression and mutual understanding. Delegation of the EU to Korea together with the Member States' embassies and other European culture focused institutions based in Korea, work to widespread European cultural values and promote cooperation in the field of culture between European and Korean counterparts.

The Protocol on cultural cooperation under the EU-Korea FTA signed in 2010, provides the legal basis for the cooperation on cultural issues. By granting preferential treatment for market access for their co-production, the protocol emphasizes importance of the audio-visual sector. Thus, number of initiatives such as European-Korean film festivals, joint art exhibition and theatrical co-productions has increased significantly since 2010. Promotion of European culture in Korea is also supported by Creative Europe program with a budget of EUR 1.46 billion. The program was launched in 2014 with the aim of facilitating cross-border exchange and cooperation in the field of culture.

Similarly, the EU National Institutes for Culture (EUNIC), which is the network of European national institutes of culture and institutions involved in promotion of European culture in counties outside Europe. The EUNIC has been deeply engaged in organizing film festivals, individual film screenings and concerts in Korea. 32 Korean Cultural Centres which are financed by the Korean government run their programs in the world including 8 in EU Member States: Belgium, France, Germany, Hungary, Italy, Poland, Spain, UK by 2019. The mission of those centres is to promote Korean culture and encourage foreigners to learn Korean language. Similarly, established in 2012 The King Sejong Institute Foundation (KSIF) is dedicated to promoting Korean culture and history through the Korean language. there are 25 King Sejong Institutes operates in 15 EU countries (Belgium, Bulgaria, Czech Republic, Estonia, Finland, France, Germany, Hungary, Italy, Latvia, Lithuania, Poland, Portugal, Spain, UK) by 2019.

Lastly, some EU Member States have been engaged in cultural collaboration with North Korea. A concert of North Korean classical musicians conducted by a South Korean conductor Myung-Whun Chung that took place in Paris in March 2012 was unprecedented example of trilateral cooperation between France and two Koreas.[32]

32) Olivier Bellamy, "Un Concert À Paris Pour Réunir Les Deux Corée," *Huffington Post* 2016. (accessed: March 10, 2019)

IV. EU's Political Relations with Two Koreas

1. EU's Political Relations with South Korea

(South) Korea has boosted its international position not only in economic dimension as a trade partner, but also in political dimension. The KOF political globalization index[33] captures the membership in international inter-governmental organizations, the number of international treaties which are signed and ratified by a country, the number of embassies across the world and participation in the UN Security Council missions. Scores range from 0 to 100, 100 indicating a very high degree of political globalization and political international integration. It shows the evolution of Korea over the last four decades indicating a clear upward trend.

In this context, Korea was assigned as one of the ten Strategic Partners of the EU together with the US, China, Japan, Brazil, Russia, India, Canada, Mexico and South Africa. The instrument of the Strategic Partnership represents the EU's response to an increasingly interdependent world, since cooperation with key powers is necessary to ensure that the EU's values and interests are preserved at the global level.

The origin of the Strategic Partnership between EU and Korea is rooted in over 50-year history as diplomatic relations between

33) Savina Gygli et al., "The Kof Globalisation Index–Revisited," *The Review of International Organizations* (2018).

The KOF Globalization Index of Korea

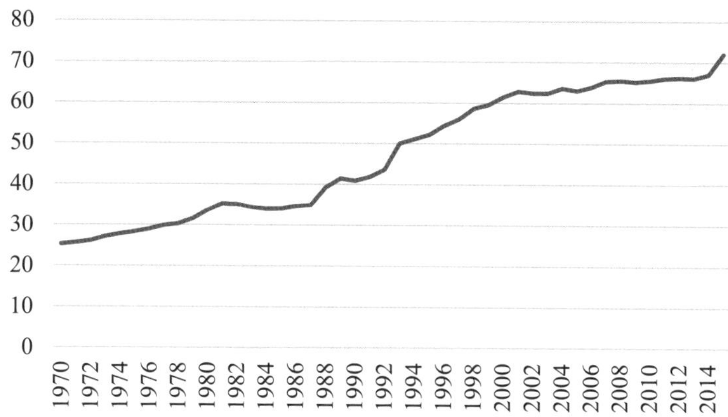

the predecessor of the EU - the EEC and Korea were established in 1963 and the permanent Korea's mission to the EEC was set up in 1965.[34] Tightening of political ties was enhanced by rapid advance of economic exchange in 1990s. As a result, the EU and Korea signed a Framework for Trade and Cooperation (which was ratified in 2001) and a Joint Declaration on Political Dialogue in October 1996. Those documents laid formal foundation for systematic economic as well as political collaboration. Furthermore, in 1997 the EU became an executive board member of KEDO which transformed bilateral cooperation to regional scope. The new political framework was signed again in 2010 and replaced the one from 1996. The document adjusted systematic framework for cooperation in order to strengthen collabo-

34) Cumings, *Korea's Place in the Sun : A Modern History.*

ration in all areas of bilateral and global issues that included, except economic cooperation also cultural, social and administrative aspects.

The two partners have held many summits since 2002: Copenhagen in 2002, Hanoi in 2004, Helsinki in 2006, Seoul in 2009, Brussels in 2010, Seoul in 2012, Brussels in 2013, Seoul in 2015 and in Brussels in 2018. Summits usually take place alongside ASEM meetings and the leaders often meet and discuss bilateral relations during other international events such as met the G20 summit in Cannes in 2011 and in Buenos Aires in 2018. Each of these summits further advanced the relations as is exemplified in the press releases following the summits.

In the 9th Summit in October 2018, the leaders committed to further develop the EU-Korea Strategic Partnership, which is underpinned by three concrete pillars: an enhanced Partnership and Cooperation Agreement; an ambitious FTA; and a Framework Participation Agreement for EU crisis management operations. The Summit provided an opportunity to explore further areas for cooperation within the Strategic Partnership. Discussions focused on the situation on the Korean Peninsula, the broader situation in the world, and trade relations. The Summit also provided an opportunity to initiate a Horizontal Aviation agreement and sign a Joint Statement committing to work closely together to fight against illegal, unreported and unregulated fishing.

During the summit the leaders discussed several pressing

issues on the global agenda, chief among them prospects for achieving lasting peace and security on the Korean Peninsula free of nuclear weapons and finding a comprehensive solution through diplomacy, while fully implementing the relevant UN Security Council Resolutions. The EU supports Korea's efforts and diplomatic initiatives, in particular the three inter-Korean Summits and the US-North Korea Summits, and the implementation of their outcomes. The EU sees the development of inter-Korean relations, the denuclearization of, and the establishment of a peace regime on the Korean Peninsula as vital for peace and security not only in East Asia, but for the entire world. In this context, the EU stressed the requirement for North Korea to completely, verifiably and irreversibly dismantle all its nuclear and other weapons of mass destruction, ballistic missiles and related programs and facilities.

The leaders also reiterated their commitment to maintaining close coordination on foreign and security issues. In the field of crisis management, the partners will continue the good cooperation under the EU-Korea Framework Participation Agreement, through which Korea has regularly contributed to the EU' s naval counter-piracy operation off the coast of the Horn of Africa, the EU Naval Force Operation Atalanta. Similarly, they discussed and agreed to cooperate more closely on implementing the 2030 Agenda for Sustainable Development and achieving its Sustainable Development Goals and will bolster their bilateral policy dialogue on international development issues and promote joint cooperation in areas and third countries of mutual interest, notably in Asia and Africa.

The leaders also stressed their commitment to implementing the Paris climate agreement. To translate this political commitment into concrete projects, the EU has set up a platform to exchange best practice on climate action and support the implementation of the Korean Government's Emissions Trading System to reach the goals of the Paris Agreement. The EU's Partnership Instrument also financially supports exchanges of cultural practitioners and artists from both the EU and Korea, economic cooperation between companies, as well as the promotion of research and teaching on EU-related issues in Korea, adding to the overall breadth of the relationship.

2. EU's Political Relations with North Korea

Most of the EU countries have diplomatic relations with North Korea and 7 Member States maintain permanent diplomatic mission in North Korea: Bulgaria, Czech Republic, Germany, Poland, Romania, Sweden and the UK. The EU established diplomatic relations with North Korea in May 2001.

In general, the EU supports efforts by the international community to promote peace and stability on the Korean Peninsula, especially through international initiatives to promote denuclearization and an improvement in the human rights situation in North Korea. Since 1998, the EU has been conducting regular political dialogue, the last, 14th session of this dialogue took place in Pyongyang in June 2015. The scope of discussions during the meeting covered all the issues of concern to the EU and the international community: non-proliferation (nuclear/Weapon of Mass Destruction and ballistic missile programs), regional stability and security, and the respect of human rights. Socio-economic issues, including the humanitarian situation in North Korea, and prospects of the EU-North Korea relations were also addressed.

The exchange of views was said to be frank and comprehensive. The political dialogue is an integral part of the EU's policy of critical engagement towards North Korea which aims at contributing to achieve peace and stability on the Korean Peninsula, upholding the international non-proliferation regime and improving the respect of human rights. The EU External Action delegation urged North Korea to re-engage in meaningful terms with the international community on all issues of concern and expressed the EU's interest to further develop bilateral relations if substantial progress on those issues is achieved.

The EU has been involved in providing assistance to some of the most vulnerable communities in North Korea since 1995. Current activities are mainly oriented towards support for the agricultural sector and are financed under the Food Security Thematic Programme of the Development Cooperation Instrument. Projects are implemented by European teams working with local partner organizations.

Officially, the EU top political bodies such as European Council and Council of the EU maintain that the continuing nuclear and ballistic missile-related activities of North Korea represent a serious threat to international peace and security. For the EU these activities undermine the global non-proliferation and disarmament regime of which the EU has been a persistent supporter for decades. In this context, the EU has implemented the restrictive measures imposed through resolutions of the UN Security Council and has reinforced them through its own measures. These measures target the North Korea's weapons of mass destruction and ballistic missile-related programs.

The EU first introduced restrictive measures against North Korea in December 2006. Those measures implemented the UN sanctions regime, which was adopted following the North Korea's claim that it had conducted a nuclear weapon test. The EU also reinforced the UN sanctions regime by adopting autonomous measures complementing and reinforcing the UN Security Council resolutions. Since 2006 the EU has adopted more than 30 restrictive measures against North Korea or North Korean citizens aligned with the UN Security Council sanctions or autonomously.

The EU-North Korea trade volume is negligible, mostly due to sanction regime imposed on the country and given its very small volume that does not even feature on the website of the Commission's Directorate-General for External Trade. The EU has regularly raised the human rights situation in North Korea bilaterally and through UN bodies, including co-sponsoring country resolutions.

V. Conclusions

From the economic perspective, the EU is the 3rd largest trading partner of Korea and Korea is the 8th largest of the EU; annual trade in goods between the EU and Korea is now worth about EUR 100 billion. The flourishing trade between them increased more than 30% from 2010 to 2015. Aside from promoting free, fair, and rules-based trade, both actors are committed to multilateral trading system and acting against protectionism. However, the export of European services to Korea counted of only 1.1% of total trade in services. This marginal number indicates some significant challenges in service exchange from Europe to Korea and clearly shows unexplored opportunities for European services, especially in legal areas.

Despite the successful implementation of the EU-Korea FTA, there is still a need for companies to operate in a more business friendly and comfortable environment - private companies have continued to complain about enforcement by some Korean government agencies, especially in area of taxation and custom regulations. Both Koreas, as well as the EU should commit more thoroughly to apply the FTA respectively to its charter and enhance bilateral exchange in services. Furthermore, with the commencement of the fourth industrial revolution more sophisticated deals and agreements are anticipated. In this regard, as much as the current FTA was ambitious and sophisticated at the time it was concluded, it may not address developing challenges in the foreseeable future which may create a need for more up-to-date bilateral, or multilateral agreements.

From the political perspective, current political arrangement serves as a platform for exchange and cooperation and is sustained alongside thriving economic collaboration. Relations between the EU and Korea are governed by three key agreements: The Framework Agreement, the FTA and the Framework Participation Agreement. The Framework Agreement is the first of its kind between the EU and an Asian country, providing a comprehensive legal framework covering a wide spectrum of policy fields. The EU and Korea cooperate closely bilaterally, regionally and globally, including cooperation on challenges such as climate change, and in formats such as the G20, and ASEM.

The Framework Participation Agreement forms the basis for Korea's participation in the EU crisis management operations. Korean naval forces are regularly participating in the EU-led Atalanta mission combating piracy in the Horn of Africa. The partners have a strong joint interest in achieving lasting peace and stability on the Korean Peninsula free of nuclear weapons, finding a comprehensive solution through diplomacy and fully implementing the relevant UN Security Council Resolutions.

Furthermore, the EU and Korea keep strengthening their

cooperation in the fight against illegal unreported and unregulated fishing, and will continue their cooperation to improve global ocean governance and to promote a sustainable blue economy at international, regional and national level. Both actors are reinforcing their climate-related cooperation to advance the international climate negotiations process based on the Paris Agreement. The EU has been working with Korea on technical cooperation on an Emission Trading System, contributing to Korea's plans to reduce its greenhouse gas emissions by 37% by 2030. The EU-Korea Development Cooperation Dialogue is one of the oldest policy dialogues with Korea and recently Korea has expressed its interest in exploring the possibility of participating in the EU Trust Funds and the EU External Investment Plan.

With its adherence to liberal values and multilateralism the EU could play much more active role towards North Korea. Current 'critical engagement' policy is aligned with the US 'maximum pressure and engagement' and encompasses negative sanctions on North Korea as a respond to its development of nuclear and missile program. Although Europe is not directly affected by the North Korean nuclear capability and missiles, 23 out of 28 current EU Member States are also NATO members. A potential attack on any NATO member, namely the US would invoke Article 5 of the NATO which says: "that an armed attack against one or more of them in Europe or North America shall be considered an attack against them all". Thus, EU Member States do have security interest, even in geographically distant

Korean Peninsula. It can be also anticipated that North Korean weapons could be obtained by other states or non-state actors such as terrorist group and such a development would threaten European security in a more direct way.

The EU involvement in peace and stability in the Korean Peninsula is further enhanced by the EU's commitment to the universal values of democracy, human rights, and the rule of law. Currently, the EU adheres to the denuclearization-first development, before any further engagement with North Korea could take place. However, the unified Europe as a raising power in multilateral arrangement could play more independent and different role then the US. The EU could counter-balance to the US policy toward North Korea and engage itself in spreading transitional universal values through non-political cooperation initiatives such as people-to-people exchange, science diplomacy, sport diplomacy and cultural exchange.

The EU's current relative success in peaceful integration of more than 500 million people was reinforced by the Helsinki process that led to the implementation of the Helsinki Agreements (1975): the accords signed by 35 European countries - communist, non-communist, and neutral ones. The agreement outlined the principles to guide East-West relations during the Cold War, including economic, scientific, cultural, and technological cooperation. They inscribed the obligation of all the signatories to respect fundamental rights such as freedom of thought, religion, and conscience. The lesson of Helsinki Accords should not be forgotten and could be applied by the EU towards North Korea and the EU's transnational engagement might contribute to the regional integration in Northeast Asia.

Chapter 2. Development of the Law for the Relation between Korea and Eastern Europe: The Legal Infrastructure on the Korea-Visegrád Relationship

Development of the Law for the Relation between Korea and Eastern Europe: The Legal Infrastructure on the Korea-Visegrád Relationship

Bongchul Kim

I. Introduction

Korea became one of the main trading partners to some Eastern European countries outside the European region. For example, Korea is one of the biggest investors in the Czech Republic since 1993 and a significant source of income through tourism. The cultural and promotional activities are also increasing with the economic partnership. Among the Eastern European countries, the Visegrád Group shows the efforts of four Central European countries – the Czech Republic, Hungary, Poland, and Slovakia – to join forces in the struggle for common goals within the all-European integration.

Korea and the Group are recently expanding new fields for their cooperation. Many activities for the cooperation which were held by Korea and the Eastern European countries were mainly based on their bilateral agreements. However, the Korea-EU Free Trade Agreement (FTA) has changed the paradigm of their cooperation. It is because the FTA provides many types of preferential rules for the trade and economic cooperation between the parties. Special commitments by partners have been made to abolish trade barriers in many sectors.

Although Korea has many international agreements in the international society for various purposes, it has built the FTA relations with various partners so far with many countries. The government of Korea expected that FTAs could work as the vehicle in promoting their trade expansion and economic growth and leap into more advanced economy. These international agreements are not just for the economic or trade benefits of this country. It also intended to utilize FTAs for the systemic reforms in several areas including its' domestic laws. In fact, Korea has improved many rules and regulations in accordance to the international standards after adopting the FTA policy. Then, the FTAs of Korea have also provided huge influence to other international laws in this country.

The main purpose of this chapter is to discuss the laws on the cooperation of Korea and the Visegrád Group as the important countries in the Eastern European region. It will start from the analysis of the three basic agreements between Korea and EU, then moves to the bilateral agreements of the Group countries with Korea. The legal analysis will be directly related to the suggestion of new possible meanings of the agreements. The laws can be significant new engines to boost better cooperation between the partners.

II. The Laws of the Korea-EU Level

1. Preferential Trade Laws: The Korea-EU FTA

The EU has developed many special or preferential rules for their internal and external trade regulations. The establishment of EU itself originated from several preferential trade agreements (PTAs) such as FTAs and the European tradition is still ruling the internal economic exchanges. Many other preferential laws are used for the trades of the EU members with non-EU members. The EU's preferential agreements with many African and Caribbean countries are good examples for this external trade regulation. Turkey is also one of the external preferential trade partners of EU.

With the sensitive and complicated political issues, the economic power and strategic value of the East Asian area has brought a new dimension to the globalising world of the twenty-first century. The trades of the East Asian countries such as China, Japan and Korea are basically regulated by the WTO rules. However, these countries opened to the preferential trade laws in 2000s. The countries are commonly establishing their own PTA rules with many partners all over the world now.

China has built PTA relationships with many countries such as Pakistan, Korea, ASEAN and even Taiwan. This big country plans to play a leading role in building the China-oriented economic cooperation structure.[1] The difficulties of WTO multinational negotiations stimulated Japan to take their own PTA policy. The county signed several bilateral Economic Partnership Agreements (EPAs) with the ASEAN members and subsequently established the comprehensive EPA with the Southeast Asian group (AJCEP Agreement). Korea intended to utilise their PTAs in promoting qualitative growth of the economic system after the Asian Financial Crisis in the late 1990s. The counterparties of the Korean PTAs are from around the world such as Chile, the US, the EU, the ASEAN, India, Australia and China.

The economic relation between Korea and the EU is based on the bilateral FTA. Negotiations on the FTA were launched in May 2007 in Seoul. After eight formal rounds of talks, the FTA was initialled by both sides on 15 October 2009. On 6 October 2010 the Agreement was officially signed during the EU-Korea Summit in Brussels. The Agreement has been provisionally applied since 1 July 2011. Then, the Korea-EU FTA became the fundamental legal tool to provide more favourable environments regarding their economic relation.

The Korea-EU FTA is the most ambitious trade agreement

1) Juliana W Chen, "Achieving Supreme Excellence: How China Is Using Agreements with Asean to Overcome Obstacles to Its Leadership in Asian Regional Economic Integration," *Chi. J. Int'l L.* 7 (2006): 660-62.

ever negotiated by the EU and it is also the EU's first trade deal with an Asian country. Furthermore, this international bilateral trade law is the first major EU trade agreement concluded after the introduction of the new strategy Global Europe, and the economic cooperation between the two partners based on the FTA has been improved in many ways.[2]

The Korea-EU FTA document consists of 15 chapters, several annexes and appendixes, three protocols and four understandings.[3] Chapter 1 and 2 set forth the objectives with some definitions and the elimination of the barriers to trade in goods. Chapter 3 provides the use of trade remedies such as safeguards. Then, Chapter 4 and 5 intend to reduce obstacles as technical trade barriers and the negative effects of Sanitary and Phytosanitary Measures. Chapter 6 and 7 aim to enhance cooperation in trade facilitation matters, and the liberalisation of trade in services or non-service sectors including telecommunications and transport.

Chapter 8 is the regulation of the freely convertible currency sector with the safeguards in the area and Chapter 9 contains a provision to enhance access to government procurement. Chapter 10 and 11 include strong disciplines in important area as the intellectual property rights and the competition regula-

---

2) Edita Śedová and David Müller, "European Union-Korea Free Trade Agreement", *Czech Yearbook of Public & Private International Law Vol. 3* (2012): 274.

3) European Union, The EU-Korea Free Trade Agreement in practice (2011): 3.

tions. Chapter 12 provides strong transparency commitments in order to an efficient and predictable regulatory environment for economic operators, especially small ones doing business in their territories. Chapter 13 provides the regulations for the promotion of sustainable development in order to strengthen their trade relations and cooperation. It contains firm commitments to multilateral labour and environmental standards by both parties. Chapter 14 has provisions on the dispute settlement. Chapter 15 is about Institutional, General and Final provisions.

Three protocols are included in the FTA to support the main document. They are Protocol on Mutual Administrative Assistance in Custom Matter, Protocol on Cultural Cooperation and Protocol on Croatian Accession. Although the FTA rules are mainly for the common economic benefits of the partners, this international law sometimes provides indirect economy related regulations. For example, the Protocol on Cultural Cooperation is to implement the protection and promotion of the diversity of cultural expressions in accordance with the UNESCO Convention. Even if the FTA is more focused on the economic interests of the parties, these protocols may have possibilities to be connected with other non-economic areas. The partners can develop the legal infrastructure for other (non-economic) purposes.

2. The Law for Other Issues and General Cooperation: The Korea-EU FA

The EU-East Asian relations for other issues are regulated by many international laws. There are several international laws for the purpose. For example, the Korea-EU Framework Agreement (FA) was signed in 1996. Now, the amendment of the FA in 2010 proclaimed a strategic partnership between the two. This FA was basis for the establishment of the Korea-EU FTA later.

The new version of the FA was signed in May 2010 and entered into force on June 1 2014. The enhanced 2010 EU-Korea FA provides the basis for strengthened cooperation and dialogue in various areas. It addresses a wide range of international concerns including non-proliferation of weapons of mass destruction, human rights, cooperation in the fight against terrorism, climate change, energy security and development assistance. The agreement will also promote cooperation in sectors vital to economic growth, such as science and technology, innovation, education and environment.

The FA consists of 10 Titles (chapters) with 53 articles and a technical sub-rule. Title I provides the basis and scopes of the cooperation with Article 1 and 2. Title II is about the dialogue and cooperation on the political issues such as 'Countering the proliferation of Weapons of Mass Destruction' (Article 4) and 'The most serious crimes of concern to the international community' (Article 6). Title III is on the cooperation in regional and international organisations. The Parties promise each other to cooperate and exchange views in regional and international fora and organizations such as the s Nations (UN), the International Labour Organisation (ILO), the Organization for Economic Co-operation and Development (OECD), the WTO, the Asia-Europe Meeting (ASEM) and ASEAN Regional Forum (ARF).

Title IV provides many articles on the economic and development cooperation. The topics of the articles in this title are Trade and investment (Article 9), Economic policy dialogue (Article 10), Business cooperation (Article 11), Taxation (Article 12), Customs (Article 13), Competition policy (Article 14), Information society (Article 15), Science and technology (Article 16), Energy (Article 17), Transport (Article 18), Maritime transport policy (Article 19) and Consumer Policy (Article 20). They are one of the important parts in this agreement and also directly related to the philosophy of the Korea-EU FTA. Some provisions even regulate the economic or trade issues that are not directly ruled by the Korea-EU FTA.

Title V is on the sustainable development issue. The articles in this title are Health (Article 21), Employment and social affairs (Article 22), Environment and natural resources (Article 23), Climate change (Article 24), Agriculture, rural development and forestry (Article 25), Marine and fisheries (Article 26) and Development assistance (Article 27). The Parties try to follow the international trends regarding this issue providing some international rules such as the Paris Declaration of 2005 on Aid Effectiveness.

Furthermore, the mainstream of this title is harmonized with the concept of the Sustainable Development Goals (SDGs) by the UN in 2015. Title VI provides regulations to the areas of education and culture. This title can be deeply related to the protocol on cultural cooperation in the Korea-EU FTA.

Title VII is the agreement on the cooperation in the area of justice, freedom and security. Based on the concept of 'Rule of law' (Article 30), the parties agree to cooperate in many issues such as Legal cooperation (Article 31), Personal data protection (Article 32), Migration (Article 33), Combating illicit drugs (Article 34), Combating organised crime and corruption (Article 35), Combating money laundering and terrorism financing (Article 36), Combating cyber-crime (Article 37) and Law enforcement cooperation (Article 38). Then, the agreement expands its regulation boundary to the fields of Tourism, Civil Society, Public administration and even Statistics area in Title VIII. Title IX and Title X include the articles on the institutional framework and final provisions.

3. The Security Issues and the related Laws: The Framework Agreement for the Participation of Korea in EU crisis Management Operations

The European and the East Asian region have some common sensitive issues. Nearly all EU members have been affected by terrorism and tackling it has never been easy. Although this issue was a bit far from the original purpose of the EU, many cases regarding terrorism stimulate the European security issue. This security issue in the East Asia is already their traditional one to the members. For example, the North Korean nuclear issue and some territorial disputes in this area may make effect to the importance. Then, the security issue to the EU-East Asian relation is also becoming more important than before.

The Agreement establishing a framework for the participation of Korea in EU crisis management operations, also called as 'Framework Participation Agreement aimed at facilitating Korea's future participation in EU Common Security and Defence Policy (CSDP) operations' was signed at Seoul on 23 May 2014. The crisis management operations agreement specifies third party invitation to participate in an EU crisis management operation. It also sets the status of Korean personnel who will be dispatched to command elements in case the CSDP operation is implemented.

The agreement consists of just 4 sections with 16 articles. Section I has 4 articles on 'Decisions relating to participation', 'Framework', 'Status of personnel and forces of the Republic of Korea' and 'Classified information' as general provisions. They provide the mainstream or the general procedures of the co-works in this field. According to the provisions in this section, the Parties will exchange their information and decision on the invitation and the contribution, and even the costs or budgets of the works.

Section II and III are the rules on civilian and military types of the EU crisis management operations. Section II is about the participation in the EU civilian crisis management operations. Article 5 provides the regulations on the 'Personnel seconded to an EU civilian crisis management operation' issue and Article 6 lays the regulations on the issue of the 'Chain of command.' Article 7 and 8 are the provisions on the 'Financial aspects' and the 'Contribution to operational budget.'

Section III (Article 9 to 12) is for the rule of the participation in the EU military crisis management operations, and the main structure of the articles is very similar to the previous section. According to the provisions of these sections, the EU control the Personnel seconded by Korea to an EU crisis management operation. The Korean government shall appoint a National Contingent Point of Contact (NPC, for the EU civilian crisis management operations) and a Senior Military Representative (SMR, for the EU military crisis management operations) to represent its national contingent in the operations.

Then, Section IV is the package of the final provisions. Here, Article 13 is for the 'Arrangements to implement the Agreement' and Article 14 is on the issue of 'Non-compliance.' Article 15 is on the 'Dispute settlement' and Article 16 provides the regulation of the 'Entry into force, Duration, and Termination.'

III. Multinational Laws and Bilateral Laws by the Member Countries of Each Party

1. Multinational Laws for Korea, EU and its Members

Although the Korea-EU trade relation has been developed mainly based on the Korea-EU FTA, the partner countries can also use the WTO multinational laws for their trade and economic issues as they are commonly the WTO members. Since 1990s, the WTO system is one of the most important international trade and economic organizations. It generally controls the international economic trend. It also provides the good decisions to the trade issues. Therefore, the WTO rules may provide general and basic regulations for the fundamental relation of them under the whole membership of the WTO.

The package of WTO agreements is general legal tool for the trade in the international stage. The WTO's agreements are the outcome of the Uruguay Round negotiations which included a major revision of the original General Agreement on Tariffs and Trade (GATT). The Uruguay Round also created many other laws for dealing with trade in services, relevant aspects of intellectual property, dispute settlement, and trade policy reviews.

Multilateral international laws may sometimes have the connecting provisions with the bilateral or internal laws which can be made by the members in the multilateral structure. These rules have the function to make the mechanism between the multilateral law and the bilateral or internal laws. For example, the WTO system provides fundamental rules for the function of FTAs. When a WTO member enters into an FTA through which it grants more favourable conditions to its trade with other WTO member parties to that agreement than to other WTO members' trade, it basically departs from the non-discrimination principle defined in Article I of GATT and other rules.

However, WTO members can enter into such FTAs under specific conditions, which are spelled out in three sets of rules: *Article XXIV of the GATT; The so-called Enabling Clause; Article V of the GATS.*[4] The Korea-EU FTA is based on Article XXIV of the GATT and other related WTO rules. Therefore, the two partners of the bilateral FTA and the WTO members, Korea and EU, have justifiable exceptions to provide favourable trade conditions from the major principle of the multilateral WTO rules.[5]

Various types of UN laws can also be applied to them in other fields. Recently, many members of the EU have regarded the issues of terrorism or refugees as serious problems in the area. Considering North Korea, (South) Korea is also very sensitive to the issues, thus it can be treated as a common topic for

4) Sung-Hoon Park, "Regionalism, Open Regionalism and Article Xxiv Gatt: Conflicts and Harmony," *Regional and global regulation of international trade* (2002): 275.
5) L Alan Winters, "Preferential Trading Agreements: Friend or Foe?," *Preferential Trade Agreements: A Law and Economics Analysis* (2011): 7.

their official talks in the EU-Korea relation. The UN rules can regulate the sensitive issues as general and fundamental laws in the international community. The partners will do some joint works for the issues based on the UN regulations and laws. Furthermore, the EU members and Korea can use many other multilateral international laws for their common issues if they are contracting parties.

2. Bilateral Agreements by Korea and Visegrád Members

Each country in the membership may have bilateral rules for the details of their trade issues. These bilateral agreements by member countries can provide specific favours to the partner countries. However, the establishment of the bilateral laws must be permitted by the EU internal law under the EU system. It can be another legal issue to study.

The first steps toward the establishment of official diplomatic relations between Poland and Korea were taken even before Poland had fully adopted democracy. After boycotting the Olympic Games in Montreal (1976), Moscow (1980) and Los Angeles (1984), the international sports community was tired of mixing sports with international politics and was determined to participate in the Seoul Olympic Games (1988).

Polish representation was accompanied by diplomats from the Ministry of Foreign Affairs at this chance. This idea of founding ties between Poland and Korea was especially supported by the Minister of Sport and Youth and president of the Polish Olympic Committee at the time, Aleksander Kwaśniewski who later became Polish President and served two terms, 1995-2005. The Polish diplomats met with their Korean counterparts at the Plaza Hotel on 30 October 1988.[6]

As a result of this meeting, the Polish Chamber of Foreign Trade opened an office in Seoul in April 1989, while the Korea Trade and Promotion Agency (KOTRA) launched the Korean Business Centre in Warsaw. These initial steps, followed by further political meetings, enhanced bilateral relations, which finally led to the establishment of diplomatic relations between Poland and Korea on 1 November 1989. The first tangible outcome of this agreement was USD 450 million loan for Poland, out of which USD 50 million aid credit was loaned on very agreeable conditions. This loan served as a basis to develop bilateral trade. Permanent diplomatic missions were also established in Warsaw and Seoul.

Since then, Poland and Korea have managed the strong economic ties through trade and private investment. Korean investment in Poland rapidly increased during the 1990s and Poland is the biggest investment destination for Korean companies in Eastern Europe and the 5 largest in the EU. Korea is one of the top 20 foreign investors in Poland, second biggest from Asia. More than 130 Korean companies in Poland creating more than

---

6) Andrzej Majkowski, "Geneza Nawiązania Stosunków Dyplomatycznych Między Polską a Republiką Korei." *Azja-Pacyfik* (2000):132-35.

20,000 jobs and the total Korean investment in Poland reached USD 1.26 billion at a peak. Over 90% of Korean investment are in the field of manufacturing sectors such as electronics, chemicals, and automobiles and car parts. This creates various spill-over effects, in addition to direct economic contribution, including the transfer of technology and managerial know-how.

Although several Korea-EU agreements such as the FTA may regulate many issues between Korea and the EU countries, the bilateral agreements by Korea and Poland are still useful. It is because they provide details of the regulation for the benefits of the partners based on the different background of each Group member. The bilateral laws can cover some areas which the FTA or FA cannot regulate. Many bilateral agreements between Korea and Poland have established for the cooperation as below;

- *Agreement between the Government of the Polish People's Republic and the Government of the Republic of Korea for the Promotion and Reciprocal Protection of Investments (1989)*
- *Convention between the Government of the Republic of Poland and the Government of the Republic of Korea for the Avoidance of Double Taxation and the Prevention of Fiscal Evasion with Respect to Taxes on Income (1991)*
- *Agreement between the Government of the Republic of Poland and the Government of the Republic of Korea for Air Service (1991)*
- *Cultural Agreement between the Government of the Republic*

of Poland and the Government of the Republic of Korea (1993)

- *Agreement between the Government of the Republic of Poland and the Government of the Republic of Korea on Scientific and Technological Cooperation (1993)*
- *Visa-Waiver Agreement between the Government of the Republic of Poland and the Government of the Republic of Korea (1993)*
- *Agreement between the Government of the Republic of Poland and the Government of the Republic of Korea on the Mutual Recognition and Exchange of International and Domestic Driving Licences (1998)*
- *Agreement between the Government of the Republic of Poland and the Government of the Republic of Korea on Co-operation and Mutual Assistance in Customs Matters (1999)*
- *Agreement on tourism cooperation between the Government of the Republic of Poland and the Government of the Republic of Korea (2004)*
- *Agreement on economic cooperation between the Government of the Republic of Poland and the Government of the Republic of Korea (2004)*
- *Agreement on social security between the Republic of Poland and the Republic of Korea (2009)*
- *Agreement between the Government of the Republic of Poland and the Government of the Republic of Korea on the Protection of Classified Military Information (2009)*
- *Protocol between the Government of the Republic of Poland*

and the Government of the Republic of Korea Amending the Convention between the Government of the Republic of Poland and the Government of the Republic of Korea for the Avoidance of Double Taxation and the Prevention of Fiscal Evasion with Respect to Taxes on Income, Signed at Seoul on the 21st Day of June 1991(2013)

- *Agreement between the Government of the Republic of Poland and the Government of the Republic of Korea on Co-operation in the Field of Defence (2013)- Agreement between the Government of the Republic of Poland and the Government of the Republic of Korea on a Working Holiday Programme (2018)*

Korea and the Czech Republic established the installation agreement of the bilateral trade office, which was signed in 1989. The KOTRA trade building was established in Prague in 1990 under the agreement. Their bilateral economic relationship has developed. The trade volume of the Eastern European country with Korea in 2006 was more than USD 800 million, which shows a 10 times larger amount than the one of 1993.

With the Korea-EU FTA since 2011, the exportation quantity of products made in Korea toward the Czech Republic has increased by 45.3%. The Korean car brand, Hyundai, built its first production factory in the Czech Republic and started its serial production in November 2008, recording a production capacity of more than 200,000 cars a year. Furthermore, Korean Air acquired shares of 44% in the Czech Airlines in 2013 in an attempt to make Prague Airport as the European distribution hub.

The bilateral agreements between Korea and the Czech Republic are also very useful for their cooperation. The bilateral agreements by the two countries are the legal infrastructure of the cooperation because the laws may provide very details for the regulation of the work areas. They are still expanding the areas of the bilateral agreements for more cooperation. The bilateral agreements between Korea and the Czech Republic have established since 1990 as below;[7)]

- *Agreement between the Government of the Czech and Slovak Federal Republic and the Government of the Republic of Korea on aviation service (1990)*
- *Agreement on trade and economic cooperation between the Government of the Czech and Slovak Federal Republic and the Government of the Republic of Korea (1990)*
- *Agreement between the Government of the Czech and Slovak Federal Republic and the Government of the Republic of Korea for the promotion and reciprocal protection of investments (1992)*
- *Convention between the Czech and Slovak Federal Republic and the Republic of Korea for the avoidance of double taxa-*

7) Bongchul Kim, "The Legal Tools for the Economic Cooperation between Korea and the Czech Republic" in Jaewan Moon and Michal Tomasek, "Law Crossing Eurasia: From Korea to the Czech Republic", *rw&r Science & New Media* (2015): 194-95.

tion ant the prevention of fiscal evasion with respect to taxes on income (1992)

- *Agreement between the Government of the Czech Republic and the Government of the Republic of Korea on waiver of visas* (1994)
- *Agreement between the Government of the Czech Republic and the Government of the Republic of Korea on cultural cooperation* (1994)
- *Agreement between the Government of the Czech Republic and the Government of the Republic of Korea on the cooperation in science and technology* (1995)
- *Agreement between the Government of the Czech Republic and the Government of the Republic of Korea on the cooperation for peaceful use of nuclear energy* (2001)
- *Arrangement between the Ministry of Education, Youth and Sport of the Czech Republic and the Ministry of Culture and Tourism of the Republic of Korea on Cooperation in the Field of Youth for 2003-2005* (2003)
- *Arrangement between the Ministry of Informatics of the Czech Republic and the Ministry of Information and Communication of the Republic of Korea on Cooperation in the Field of Information and Communication Technologies* (2004)
- *Arrangement between the Ministry of Industry and Trade of the Czech Republic and the Ministry of Foreign Affairs and Trade of the Republic of Korea on Economic Cooperation* (2009)
- *Agreement between the Czech Republic and the Republic of*

Korea concerning a Working Holiday Program (2011)

3. The Three Layers of the International Laws: The Relationship and the Functions of the Laws

With the multilateral international laws which Korea and the EU members signed in the international community, the partners may make bilateral rules which can be applied only on the Korea-EU level as mentioned above. In this case, many of the legal points in the Korea-EU agreements such as the FTA and FA can be based on the principles of the multilateral international laws. However, these bilateral laws may provide some specific promises with the legal basis only for the partners.

Therefore, the multinational laws which was mentioned above and the bilateral laws are under the legal principle of the 'general and special laws relation'. Special laws can be firstly applied to a certain issue than general laws under the principle if the special laws do not have different rules. A certain regulation by a special law which is different from the regulation of general laws can be applied for the parties of the special law. Of course, multilateral international laws may have the permission provisions for the possibility of the 'special law' in their structure as explained above.

On the other hand, the Korea-EU bilateral laws have the provisions to connect the law to the multilateral laws. For example, the Title III of the Korea-EU FA provides the issue of the cooperation in regional and international organisations as mentioned above. The articles in this title are on the cooperation in regional and international organizations such as the ASEAN and the UN and the WTO. That means the Korea-EU agreement is directly related to the multilateral laws. The Korea-EU rules must be harmonized with the order of the multilateral society. This is true to the bilateral rules between Korea-EU members.

Although the Korea-EU agreements may regulate many issues between Korea and the EU countries, the other types of bilateral agreements which are made by Korea and one of the EU members are still useful. It is because these 'one-to-one style' bilateral agreements by the EU member countries with Korea can provide specific favours only to the partner countries. However, the establishment of the laws must be permitted by the EU law under the EU system.[8] The EU internal system and the related regulations are the legal bases for the agreements of the Korea-EU individual member. The laws must also be harmonised with the whole EU external regulation structure.

With respect to the legal tools for their relation, many regulations and standards under the international laws are considered as a kind of cooperation resource, namely 'Legal Infrastructure'. For example, a country that has various and sound trade regulations under the economic agreements with partners can

8) Piet Eeckhout, "The EU and its Member States in the WTO in Lorand Bartels and Federico Ortino, *Regional Trade Agreements and the Wto Legal System* (Oxford University Press, 2006), 463.

produce many types of economic benefits. Korea is equipped with many legal infrastructures which lead to sound economic growth. This point is also important in the economic cooperation under FTAs. The Korea-EU FTA can be more effectively used for the economic cooperation activities between the partners.

IV. Possible Changes and Challenges in the Law

1. The Legal Mechanism between the International Laws and the National Laws

Many (multinational or bilateral) international laws may stimulate some changes of national laws for better or more cooperation from both sides. The Korean government expected that their FTAs can be used as the 'legal infrastructures' for their recovery from the Asian Financial Crisis with the systemic reforms including the domestic laws. In fact, they have improved many types of domestic laws following the international standards with their FTAs.

There are several domestic laws and other regulations that have provisions concerning FTAs in Korea. For example, Customs Act and Act on the Investigation of Unfair International Trade Practices and Remedy against Injury to Industry (Trade Remedy Act) are the major Korean substantive laws. These national laws provide several special articles regarding their FTA issues.

Article 22-3 (Safeguard Measures by Free Trade Agreements with Foreign States), 22-4 (Abatement of Implementation of Safeguard Measures against FTA Counterparts), 22-5 (Trade Damage Support Measures on Increase in Import of Special Goods following FTA) and 22-6 (Cooperation with Foreign State after FTA) in the Trade Remedy Act are special provisions related to FTAs. There are also special laws regarding FTAs such as 'Act on Special Cases of the Customs Act for the Implementation of Free Trade Agreements'.

Many other domestic laws which have already existed and are not directly related to the Korea-EU international issues, such as FTA topics, can be changed by the establishment of the international laws. For example, the Korean government changed various domestic laws with the launching of the two major FTAs, the Korea-EU FTA and the Korea-US FTA during 2008-2012. It is because the government realized that the domestic rules had to be harmonized with the principle of the international laws. The internationalized standards in the Korean domestic laws could regulate the Korean society with the FTA environment.[9]

---

9) Bongchul Kim, "The changes of Korean Domestic Laws with the FTA system, *Chonbuk Law Rev. Vol. 44* (2015): 424-27.

The changes of Korean Domestic Laws with the two major Korean FTAs during 2008-2012

Administrative Procedures Act	2011
Postal Service Act	2011
Telecommunications Business Act	2010
Radio Waves Act	2010
Act on Regulation and Punishment of Criminal Proceeds Concealment	2008
Monopoly Regulation and Fair Trade Act	2012
Individual Consumption Tax Act	2011
Local Tax Act	2011
Act on Designation and Management of Free Trade Zones	2011
Utility Model Act	2011
Design Protection Act	2011
Unfair Competition Prevention and Trade Secret Protection Act	2011
Patent Act	2011
Pharmaceutical Affairs Act	2011
Copyright Act	2011
Trademark Act	2011
Certified Tax Accountant Act	2011
Foreign Legal Consultant Act	2009/2011
Certified Public Accountant Act	2011

Some Korean domestic laws were newly made in relevance to the substantive issue of FTAs. For instance, several laws regard the re-organisation of and the support of domestic industries that interlinked with the FTA policy. 'Special Act on Assistance to Farmers, Fishermen, etc. following the Conclusion of Free

Trade Agreements' and 'Act on Trade Adjustment Assistance Following the Free Trade Agreements.' The Act on Trade Adjustment Assistance Following the Free Trade Agreements consists of 24 articles and they are mainly regarding provisions for the support of industries which want to change their business structures or items.

There were discussions for legislation of a general law regarding processes of FTAs negotiations and their execution.[10] Act on the Conclusion Procedure and Implementation of Commercial Treaties was established in 2011 for the purpose. Under this law, many major difficulties in the decision-making process and in the implementation of FTAs can be resolved as emphasising the active role of the Korean National Assembly and the cooperation of sharing the responsibilities between the legislative and the administrative authorities.

In the point of the national laws, Korea is still in need of more legal changes to comply with the standards under the international laws and agreements. Therefore, the Korea-EU legal exchange or cooperation is also needed in this dimension. The cooperation in this sector also requires intense exchange of human resources in the field. However, it is imperative to note that the legal exchange and cooperation should be done step by step to maximize the chance of success.

---

10) Chang-Hyun Park, "The Role of the National Assembly in the Process of Trade Negotiation:, *Korea Legislation Research Institute* (2008): 177-78.

2. New Functions of the International Laws

The main function of the Korea-EU bilateral international laws has been focused on (economic) cooperation. However, the fields of their cooperation are expanding with the new function of the bilateral laws. For example, the three Korea-EU agreements can make a synergy effect for the peacekeeping or security issues in the area. The peace maintenance issue is a very serious question in the Korean Peninsula and even in the Northeast Asian area. Therefore, the international laws will be useful tools in working out the solution to this complicated and sensitive issue.

According to the Korea-EU FA Title II, the Parties will have dialogue and cooperation on the political issues such as the 'Countering the proliferation of Weapons of Mass Destruction' and 'Small Arms and Light Weapons.' These activities are to promote peaceful solutions in international or regional conflicts and the strengthening of the UN and other international organizations. Furthermore, the provisions on the 'most serious crimes of concern to the international community' and 'Cooperation in combating terrorism' can also be useful to establish the common policy on the peacekeeping issue in the area. The EU CSDP operations can be practiced in the third country and it can cover somewhere of the Northeast Asia by the decision of the EU and/or the international society. The agreement has some practical meanings for the solution to the peacekeeping problems in the Korean Peninsula.

In addition, Article 12 of the Protocol Concerning the Definition of Originating Products and Methods of Administrative Cooperation in the Korea-EU FTA provided the possibility for the special treatment of Kaesong Industrial Complex (KIC) in North Korea. Also, Annex IV of the protocol provides the details on the Committee on Outward Processing Zones (OPZs). According to provision, the Committee will discuss the criteria for OPZs like the KIC and the special treatment of the Zone under the FTA order. Korea is driving their FTAs to promote the constructive engagement with North Korea by extending trade preferences to the products from the KIC. The Korean government thought that the FTAs could be useful for the stability of the Korean Peninsula. The special treatment provisions of the FTA have the very crucial possibility to soften the political tensions in the area.[11]

The Korea-EU agreements can be used for new sensitive issues such as human rights and development assistance. Title V of the FA is on the sustainable development issue. With the accordance of the international rules such as the Sustainable Development Goals (SDGs) by the UN, the Parties will make more detailed cooperation projects under the FA rules. Of course, some provisions of the EU crisis management operations agreement can

---

11) Bongchul Kim and Ho Kim, "Analysis and Proposals to the Laws in the Kaesong Industrial Complex: For Better," *Korea Journal* 54, no. 4 (2014): 95.

be also used as indirect ways for the purpose. The FTA rules are sometimes related to human rights issues or even development issues.

For example, many FTAs have owned labour related rules in their provisions, and the working conditions at the KIC have been a subject of debate. It contains firm commitments to multilateral labour and environmental standards. If the Korean FTAs have better labour regulations in the KIC, they will be more helpful to extract some solutions for the labour environment or the human rights issues in North Korea.

To globalize the KIC with strengthening inter-Korean trade, upgrading the working condition of North Korean workers is essential.[12] Here, the European standard for the working conditions and human rights issues will provide certain direction. Even if the level is too high for the North Korean government to achieve at the moment, the Korea-EU cooperation working with the consideration of the human right issues in North Korea may make progress. In the long term view, the cooperation will provide a gate for North Korea to open.

Recently, the development issue is one of the emerging topics in Korea. The concept of Official Development Assistance (ODA) is the official assistance that advanced countries provide loans, technical aids, and others to developing countries or international organizations as parts of the development field. Although

---

12) Jay Lefkowitz, "Freedom for All Koreans," *The Wall Street Journal* 2006.

Korea recently changed its status from an aid recipient to a donor, its experience as a donor is short and the awareness of the development projects still needs to be improved.[13] The European experience in this field may provide a positive influence to the Korean development works. The EU has established the 'European styles' in the administrative, the judicial and even human rights and development fields, from many agreements and laws for the cooperation such as the Treaty of Lisbon in 2007.

Especially speaking, Korea and some Eastern European members such as the Visegrád Group can jointly do more sensitive political works in North Korea. The Group shows the efforts of four Central European countries to join forces in the struggle for common goals within the all-European integration. Then, the works will be based on the special status of the member countries (historically and practically from Western European countries) to North Korea. This is related to the point that one of the main purposes of the Group is in the security field.

Furthermore, these Eastern European countries such as Poland and Czech Republic have their own special experience on ODA issues. They can provide good advice to the Korean ODA works and develop joint projects to third countries. Of course, North Korea can be included in the group of the targets. However, when an OECD DAC inspectorate visited Seoul in 2008

13) Lee Tae Joo, "Korea Joins the Big League with a Donor-Centric Approach," *Aid and Development Effectiveness: Towards Human Rights, Social Justice and Democracy* (2010): 234.

and asked if South Korea was willing to include its assistance to North Korea in the ODA, the South Korean authority was unable to provide a definite answer. This ambiguous situation remains unresolved and it must be politically determined.[14]

3. Possible Challenges in the Future

Besides the security issue, the European area recently has many changes and/or challenges to the internal and external laws. The Brexit and the refugee issues are the examples of the recent serious points to the EU system and the laws. These issues may make the changes of the European laws and sometimes the EU external international laws.

Although the Korea-EU bilateral laws are useful for many issues, the partners have some challenging points to their laws. The challenges can be related to the changes of international trends or certain policies of the members. For example, the 'Brexit' and the refugee issues in the EU area are recent serious points to the EU system and the laws. Although anyone cannot predict the future of a certain issue, it is obvious that the Brexit issue will not only affect Europe but also the international society as a whole.[15] This is connected to the Korean future policies, too.

---

14) Sang Hwa Chung, "A Prospect for Inter-Korean Economic Development Cooperation: Utilizing Oda to Promote Multilateral Forestation Projects," *Korean Unification Studies* (2012): 125.

15) Denis MacShane, *Brexit: How Britain Left Europe* (Bloomsbury Publishing, 2016), 15.

There have been many problems in the law department as well, so the situation has resulted in the waiting of a solution. Foremost, in order to follow the law standards of the EU, the instances of the national laws of Britain and its traditional law principles will be restored. Of course, as is the case of finance, even if Britain will maintain EU's law standards, there must be an agreement among other member states.

If Britain's traditional standards are restored in any field, the judicial precedents that have already been established in Britain based on EU laws have a chance of creating confusion and chaos. This is due to that face the within the Anglo-American Law tradition which focuses on Case Law, it may be better to continue following the judicial precedents that have already followed EU law. On the other hand, the law culture of Scotland which has retained the foundation of EU Continental Law may collide with the law culture of England. This means that within the united law system of commonwealth countries between England and Scotland, there may now be differences between the Anglo-American and Continental Law traditions of England and Scotland.

The Brexit situation will have influences on the non-EU members such as Korea. On the one hand, the partnership of the Korea-EU FTA has to be changed excluding the UK. Then, other Korea-EU bilateral agreements will also face a similar situation. On the other hand, just like the FTA and law treaties signed between Korea and the UK, because the law treaties signed between the two countries do not apply, new treaties must be established.

Therefore, there will be circumstances between the partnership of Korea and the UK in regards to international law. The volatility of the domestic norms of the UK provide a variety of new problems for Korea, too. Korean industries within Britain will now have to look into British standards rather than the EU standards. These factors have a chance of resulting in higher costs than before.

These issues may make changes in the European laws and sometimes the EU external international laws. Some smaller blocks inside the EU structure can also be a part of the issue. The North Korean issue is the same example in the Korean Peninsula. Just after the announcement of the UK government regarding the start of the UK-New Zealand FTA talks, the Korean government established the task force team regarding the possible Korea-UK FTA negotiation works. The team is preparing the possible negotiation for the bilateral FTA between the two countries. Although the main contents of the FTA will be similar to the Korea-EU FTA regulations, the Korea-UK FTA can be a bit different from the Korea-EU FTA in some sensitive areas such as the finance field.

V. The Possible Works of the Visegrád Group to Korean Issues

1. The Challenge and Cooperation of the Smaller Groups in Europe and East Asia

Some smaller blocks inside the EU structure can also be a part of the issues. According to the Visegrád Declaration, the Group was established as an alliance of initially three, and later four states to further their European integration as well as upgrading their cooperation in such fields as economy, military and energy. As the member countries in the area are under pressure of EU to harmonise their financial systems towards the European standard, the economies of the members highly depend on international circumstances. The economy of the four member countries is growing fast compared with the other EU member states. The annual average of economy growth for the group is around 3.5% in recent years, while for the 28 EU members, it has remained below 2%.

The East Asian area also has similar symptom. China plans to play a leading role in building the China-oriented economic cooperation structure[16] and it is building the Regional Comprehensive Economic Partnership (RCEP) system. It is a trade

---

16) Chen, "Achieving Supreme Excellence: How China Is Using Agreements with Asean to Overcome Obstacles to Its Leadership in Asian Regional Economic Integration," 660-62.

agreement linking the ASEAN with China, Korea, Japan, India, Australia, and New Zealand. This country seems to be planning a path to major hegemony against the US using their regional integration policy. Although the main expectation of the AJCEP Agreement is the economic benefits, Japan also intended to restrain rising Chinese influence in the Southeast Asia. Japan is recently trying to be more positive on the PTAs launching and come up with many new ideas such as the development and expansion of the Trans-Pacific Partnership (TPP) system. The TPP plan by Japan is sometimes read in direct opposition to the RCEP plan by China.

A member country in each area may make more special relationship with the partner's smaller group/block for a certain reason. More recently, the trade volume between Korea and the Eastern European countries reached USD 13.7 billion in 2013. This figure makes Korean companies more and more interested in investing there. More than 330 Korean companies, including Samsung Electronics and Hyundai Motor, operate there, with their investment exceeding USD 4.9 billion in 2013. In Slovakia, which has a population of 5.5 million; Korean manufacturers employ about 27,000 workers.

The cooperation between Korea and the Group countries may also be essential in terms of leading North Korea to take a path toward reform and democracy. The experiences of the Eastern European members in regime transformation at the end of the Cold War could also be considered by North Korea as a possible reference model if it chose to take a step toward change. Korea knows that the potential of cooperation with these countries has yet to be fully achieved.

It is also important that recently the Group members are making significant steps to strengthen actual cooperation outside the economic area. In July 2014 in the Slovakian capital of Bratislava, Korea's Foreign Minister held the first meeting with his counterparts from the four-member states. One month before the summit assistant minister-level officials from the five countries gathered in Seoul for their first round of consultative talks.

2. New Roles and Legal Infrastructures of the Korea-Visegrád Group Cooperation

Many economic cooperation works by Korea and the Visegrád Group were mainly based on their bilateral agreements since the late 1980s and the early 1990s. However, the Korea-EU FTA in the late 2000s started to establish a new paradigm for their cooperation. Now the peace maintenance issue is a very serious question in the Korean Peninsula and even in the East Asian area. Therefore, international laws will be useful tools in working out the solution to this complicated and sensitive issue. The three Korea-EU agreements that previously explained can make a synergy effect for the peacekeeping or security issues in the East Asian area. The Group can and must be definitely engaged to the peacekeeping works.

First, some parts of the Korea-EU FA may provide legal solutions for the issue. According to the FA Title II, the Parties will have dialogue and cooperation on the political issues such as the 'Countering the proliferation of Weapons of Mass Destruction' and 'Small Arms and Light Weapons.' These activities are to promote peaceful solutions in international or regional conflicts and the strengthening of the UN and other international organizations. Furthermore, the provisions on the 'The most serious crimes of concern to the international community' and 'Cooperation in combating terrorism' can also be useful to establish the common policy on the peacekeeping issue in the area.

Second, the EU crisis management operations agreement is a more direct international law for the issue. The EU CSDP operations can be practiced in the third country and it can cover somewhere of the Northeast Asia by the decision of the EU and/or the international society. The Korean government may have a certain cooperation role with the EU in this case. Therefore, the agreement has some practical meanings for the solution to the peacekeeping problems in the Korean Peninsula. Of course, it must be harmonized with the common policies of the international society as the agreement confirmed.

Lastly, FTAs can be also used for the solutions on this issue. Korea is driving their FTAs to promote the constructive engagement with North Korea by extending trade preferences to the products from the Kaesong Industrial Complex (KIC) in North

Korea. Although there have been several political influences, the two Koreas consented to guarantee business environments in the KIC that meet international standards, and work towards improving the competitiveness of its products in the global market.[17]

Almost every Korean FTA has special treatment rules to recognise the products from the Complex in North Korea as (South) Korean local products. There is no such provision in the first Korean FTA, the Korea-Chile FTA. From the second Korean FTA, the Korea-Singapore FTA provided special treatments of certain goods made at the KIC. The Korea-EFTA FTA, the Korea-ASEAN FTA and the Korea-India CEPA provide similar standards for the treatment of the KIC products as the Korean product. The Korea FTAs with ASEAN, Peru and Colombia gave breaks to 100 products. Then, the Korea-China FTA expands the possibility of the special treatment to 310 products in the KIC.

Article 12 of the Protocol Concerning the Definition of Originating Products and Methods of Administrative Co-operation in the Korea-EU FTA provided the possibility for the special treatment of KIC. Then, Annex IV of the protocol provides languages about the details on the concept of the Committee on Outward Processing Zones (OPZs). The Korea-US FTA also

17) Myung-Chul Cho, "Strategies for Promoting Exports of Companies in Gaeseong Industrial Complex," *Korea Institute for International Economic Policy* (2005): 16-27.

provides a possibility of the treatment by establishing the 'Committee on Outward Processing Zones on the Korean Peninsula.' It was a concession of both parties because Korea considered the KIC as an important issue while the US worried about security problems from North Korea. It is because the Korea-EU FTA was concluded after the conclusion of the Korea-US FTA and the EU requested a similar level of concession compared with the Korea-US FTA.[18] According to provision, the Committee will discuss the criteria for OPZs like the KIC and the special treatment of the Zone under the FTA order.

The special treatment provisions of the Korean FTAs clearly have political reasons. The Korean government thought that the FTAs could be useful for the stability of the Korean Peninsula. Therefore, the special treatment rules to the KIC products in the FTAs can be read as the legal infrastructure for the economic and the political cooperation of two Koreas which are supported by the Korean FTA partners including the EU members. Korea and the Group members can jointly do more sensitive political works in North Korea. Then, the works will be based on the special status of the member countries to North Korea. This is related to the point that one of the main purposes of the Group is in the security field.

---

18) Mark E Manyin, "Imports from North Korea: Existing Rules, Implications of the Korus Fta, and the Kaesong Industrial Complex" (2011), 15.

VI. Final Remarks

The three layers of the various international rules on the relationship between Korea and the Visegrád Group are connected each other. They may have 'general and special law' relations or some rules can be applied under the boundary of the other rules. Sometimes the function of a certain law can be expanded with the others role or the purposes of the cooperation. Researchers must find out or develop the issues to cover the needs for the cooperation with the partners.

Furthermore, the international laws between them may make influences to the national laws. For example, many Korean domestic laws have changed with the Korea-EU FTA. The international-national law harmonization issue is important and it can also be related to some challenges of other factors such as the Brexit issue in the European area. The law improvement task must be done with the consideration of these changes and challenges of the law.

Many economic cooperation works by Korea and the Eastern European countries were mainly based on some multilateral laws in the international community and their bilateral agreements since the late 1980s and the early 1990s. However, the Korea-EU FTA in the late 2000s started to establish a new paradigm for their cooperation. This FTA by the Korea-EU level is significant as a legal tool for the economy and trade with the member countries. Therefore, many new legal issues will be related to the FTA.

Here, the other Korea-EU agreements such as the FA can be used for the same goal and they can even expand the fields of cooperation. For example, the Korea-EU FTA may provide some opportunities to push for openness of North Korea. The increased trade through the FTAs and globalization policy on the KIC may produce greater openness with the positive possibilities in North Korea. The new version of the FA may provide the legal basis for strengthened and direct cooperation in the North Korean issues. The Korea-EU Agreement for the participation of Korea in EU crisis management operations may also expand the partner's cooperation in the field of the security and defence regarding North Korea.

However, there are still many problems to solve in order to reach these goals. The two Korean governments are creating some opportunities to discuss their issues. The (South) Korean government also has some responsibility to improve the KIC globalizing policy. The combination of the Korean economic cooperation with the Eastern European countries such as Poland and the Czech Republic under the globalization policy of the KIC may create a synergy effect for the solutions to the problems. Regarding this point, the Group countries have special position as the middlemen between two Koreas.

Through the cooperation works with Korea, these Eastern European countries may provide many lessons from their economic and legal experiences in adjusting to the capitalism in 1990s for the Korean issues. The assists from the European countries, the Inter-Korea works may have alternative solution. Based on this cooperation, the bilateral relation between two countries can be also developed to another step. For this purpose, they can use the international laws between Korea and the countries as the 'legal infrastructures'.

The Inter-Korean cooperation projects could be considered in the effort as combination with the ODA approach. If the main part of this support is to upgrade the level of labour, environment and others, furthermore to harmonize global standards in North Korea, it would create another synergy under the possible joint ODA works of the Korea-the Group members to North Korea. Then, this cooperation will also be based on the international and national laws of them.

Chapter 3.
SMEs and Start-up Policies and Challenges: A Comparative Analysis of the EU and Korea

SMEs and Start-up Policies and Challenges: A Comparative Analysis of the EU and Korea

Hayann Lee

I. Introduction

The competitiveness of small and medium-sized enterprises (SMEs) is a core issue in the Korean economy. They account for the majority of the total businesses and almost 90% of the total employment. Thus, without improvement in the competitiveness of SMEs, it is difficult for the Korean economy to continue to grow. In addition, in order to keep moving and increase profits in the intense and expanding international labour market, more SMEs need to be incorporated into the global value chain system. This is only possible through competitive SMEs.

In 2017, the Korean government promoted the Small and Medium Business Administration to the Ministry of SMEs and Start-ups, a ministerial-level organization. Such a reorganization is based on the perception that it would be difficult to improve growth and distribution in the present Korean economy without the advancement of SMEs. Will the Ministry of SMEs and Start-ups be able to achieve increased performance over the previous one in accordance with its enhanced status? So far, since the establishment of the framework act on small and medium enterprises in 1966, all administrations have been supported SMEs. Since SMEs make up the majority of all businesses and they are politically important policy targets, SME support policies have always been one of the most important election commitments. Support for SMEs has expanded and there are a variety of types of programs in all departments. Despite this support, considering the current condition of SMEs, SME policy is actually verging on failure. Because it's been 50 years since the implementation of SME policy, it is now necessary to analyse the performance of SME policies and systems, organization, and operational methods in depth. Considering these situations, it is also necessary to analyse the revision process of SME policies and propose a future vision to meet the rapidly increasing demand for policy.

For this purpose, this chapter would like to study the case of the EU. Both Korea and the EU are not only aware of the importance of SMEs in the economy, but they also face common challenges in the establishment of SME related policies. In general, the EU and Korea regard SMEs as the foundation of the economy. SMEs play an important role in both the EU and Korean economy. The number of SMEs and the number of employees in the EU and Korea is very similar. According to Eurostat, SMEs represent 99% of all businesses in the EU. According to Korean National Statistical Office, SMEs take up 99% of number of enterprises.

The research in this chapter will examine and compare the status of SMEs, the history of policies, and SME support programs between the EU and Korea. In addition, the start-ups that will lead new technology business are attracting attention as the start of the fourth industrial revolution, and the EU fully supports them. As a result, the EU start-up market is growing fast second only to Silicon Valley in the US. We will look at the EU start up support program to discover some possible implications for Korea.

II. SME policy of the EU

1. SME policy of the EU

The EU SME policy of the early 1980s was to promote the creation of employment through the revival of SMEs as an alternative way to solve the serious unemployment problems of European countries. This began when the European Parliament and the European Commission announced the European Year of Small and Medium-sized Enterprises and Craft Industry in 1983. In the early 2000s, the EU recognized that it was important to take full advantage of the flexibility of SMEs as a way to boost the European economy.

In 2000, the Council of the European Union created a more environmentally friendly climate for SMEs and a system to directly help them with the announcement of a 10-year goal. This was the Lisbon Agenda. The goal of this policy was to make the EU a globally competitive sustainable knowledge-based society by 2010.

The primary task needed to achieve this goal was to create a standard for classifying companies. Until the mid-1990s, there were numerous classification systems for SMEs in Europe, which caused confusion among businessmen as well as government offices. To clarify this, in 2003 the European Commission created a standard for classifying companies in the EU. The following table shows the corporate classification criteria.

The definition of micro, small, and medium-sized enterprises[1]

Enterprise category	Persons employed	Annual Turn over	or	Annual balance sheet total
Medium-sized	<250	≤ EUR 50 million		≤ EUR 43 million
Small	<50	≤ EUR 10 million		≤ EUR 10 million
Micro	<10	≤ EUR 2 million		≤ EUR 2 million

1) Commission Recommendation of 6 May 2003 concerning the definition of micro, small and medium-sized enterprises. (2003, May 20). Retrieved from https://eur-lex.europa.eu/legal-content/EN/TXT/?uri=CELEX:32003H0361

The number of employees in the company and the annual sales amount divide companies into medium/small/micro-sized companies. The classification of companies above applies only to individual companies. If the company is a subsidiary of a large corporation, it should include the number of employees, sales, and balance sheet of the parent company.

The characteristics of SMEs within the EU are that they make an absolute contribution to the total number of enterprises and significantly contribute to employment and added value. Micro, small, and medium-size enterprises make up 99% of all businesses in the EU. In 2017, just under 24 million SMEs generated EUR 4 trillion in added value and employed 93 million people. This is 66% of the EUs' total employment and 56% of the total added value. Spain, Italy, France, Germany, and Britain, in that order, are the countries with a largest number of SMEs.

Another characteristic of SMEs within the EU is that 93% of them are micro businesses with fewer than nine employees. The majority of them are family businesses that are usually managed by a person who has the right of management and ownership. Since one SME representative runs the company and makes all the decisions, the management structure of SMEs is simpler and more flexible than that of large enterprises. In addition, SMEs are small in size, which creates a closer relationship with employees, suppliers, and customers. It is also worth noting that SMEs hire women and younger people more often compared to large corporations.

SMEs and large enterprises: number of enterprises, employment, and value added in 2016 in the EU-28 non-financial business sector[2]

	Micro	Small	Medium	SME	Large	Total
	Number of enterprises (millions)					
In thousands	22,232	1,392	225	23,849	45	23,894
In % of total enterprise population	93.0%	5.8%	0.9%	99.8%	0.2%	100%
	Persons employed (millions)					
In thousands	41,669	27,982	23,398	93,049	46,665	1,397,141
In % of total employment	29.8%	20.0%	16.7%	66.6%	33.4%	100%
	Value added (EUR billion)					
In EUR trillion	1,482	1,260	1,288	4,030	3,065	7,095
In % of total value added	20.9%	17.8%	18.2%	56.8%	43.2%	100%

However, there are also problems that exist. The labour productivity of SMEs is 14% lower than that of large companies, but the number of employees per corporation is 254 times larger. They often encounter challenges when confronted with the complicated administrative and legal environment due to the unified European market and globalization. Also, as they operate on a small scale, they often lack management training and,

2) Reprinted from Annual Report on European SMEs 2016/2017, by European Commission, retrieved from https://ec.europa.eu/docsroom/documents/26563/attachments/1/translations/en/renditions/pdf

as most of them are family run companies, another issue is that they do not wish to delegate management rights to people other than family members. Above all, the biggest issue is difficulty with financing. They have less access to global financial markets than large corporations that work on a global scale as well as in the unified European market. Therefore, funds are generally raised by individuals and they often have limited availability of financial resources. These problems are major growth obstacles for SMEs. Now, let's take look at the number of employees per SME and their gross added value within the EU.

Number of persons employed and Value added per employee[3)]

Enterprise category	Number of enterprise (%)	Number of persons employed (millions)	Value added per employee (EUR billion)
Micro	93.0	1.9	36.30
Small	5.8	19.9	44.83
Medium	0.9	103.1	53.99
SME	99.8	4.0	43.40
Large	0.2	1,016	64.74
Total	100	5.9	50.49

3) Reprinted from 2017 SBA Fact Sheet & Scoreboard, by European Commission, retrieved from https://ec.europa.eu/docsroom/documents/29489/attachments/1/translations/en/renditions/native

The added value of SMEs has been on the rise since the global financial crisis in 2009. And though the number of employees from SMEs has decreased, there has been an increasing trend in recent years. In order to solve these problems and to enable the EU SMEs to be competitive in the global economy, the EU recommended the following steps.

They should prioritize the abandonment of the family owned business management model, production, and marketing methods. In addition, as the EU is a single market, they must cooperate with each other in order to overcome handicaps inherent with small size companies in the supply and distribution of goods within member countries. To adapt to the rapidly changing business environment and overcome problems, they need support from trade organizations, governments, and other EU institutions. Lastly, support at the EU level was sought by creating SME laws and policies to help SMEs without giving special favour to specific companies or industries. As a result, on June 25, 2008, the Small Business Act (SBA) was announced. Next we will look at the EU Small Business Act (SBA) execution process and the Small Business Act (SBA) itself.

2. The EU「Small Business Act (SBA; Small Business Act of 2008)」

In the late 1970s, European countries began looking for ways to create jobs through SMEs in order to solve serious unemployment problems and by 1983 the foundation of the EU SME policy had already been laid. The European Commission and the European Parliament jointly announced a policy of SME promotion, which was the beginning of EU SME policy. Also, 1983 was designated as the 'European Year of Small and Medium Sized Enterprises and Craft Industry'.

Three years later, in 1986, the 'SME Action Programme' was adopted by the board of directors, which became a trigger to create an opportunity to shift public perception of SMEs. It was a plan to create a desirable environment for SMEs and help make them competitive in the global economy. At that time, Europe felt a great sense of crisis because it maintained high unemployment and low economic growth rates when compared with world powers such as the US and Japan. To overcome this, the SME Task Force, an organization to promote SMEs, was established along with the SME Action Program.

However, despite these efforts, Europe continued to experience low growth and high unemployment into the 1990s. There was an emerging opinion among the EU member countries that it was necessary to actively support and foster SMEs in order to reduce unemployment and promote economic growth. As a solution to this, the European Commission prepared SME policies by promoting the Integrated Program in favour of SMEs and Craft Sector.

As inaugurated by the EU in 1993, Article 130 of the Treaty on European Union defined new legal grounds related to corporate policy. It was based on dividing the EU corporate policy into three sections: strengthening the competitiveness of the industry through a unified market, corporate innovation support policies, and SME policies. The contents of the treaty are as follows.

Treaty of European Union, Article 130[4]

The Community and the Member States shall ensure that the conditions necessary for the competitiveness of the Community's industry exist.

For that purpose, in accordance with a system of open and competitive markets, their action shall be aimed at:

- *speeding up the adjustment of industry to structural changes;*
- *encouraging an environment favourable to initiative and to the development of undertakings throughout the Community, particularly small and medium-sized undertakings;*
- *encouraging an environment favourable to cooperation between undertakings;*
- *fostering better exploitation of the industrial potential of policies of innovation, research and technological development.*

In 1995, the European Commission submitted its corporate policy report, 'Think Small First', to the Council of Ministers, further strengthening the EU's interest in SMEs. The title of the report and the ideology of the EU SME policy, 'Think Small

4) Treaty on European Union (Maastricht text), July 29, 1992, 1992 O.J. C 191/1.

First', forms the basis for SME policies and legislation in European countries. It is also often referenced in European government policy reports, at corporate events, and in comments by politicians and policy makers. It is a catchphrase that emphasizes the importance of SMEs and a willingness to prioritize SMEs in EU policy.

Despite these efforts, until the late 2000s, SMEs in the EU were still considered to be limited by bureaucracy and competition with large corporations. Since October 2007 however, the European Commission has continuously promoted the Lisbon Agenda and enacted the Small Business Act (SBA) as part of the 'growth and employment strategy' to both realize the idea of 'Think Small First' and to establish the EU as the world's most dynamic knowledge-based economy by 2010.

Due to the global financial crisis in 2008, the policy making authority of the EU became more interested in SMEs, which further increased the need for legislation. The European Commission presented the SBA in June 2008 by collecting opinions from SME organizations such as the European Association of Craft and Small and Medium-sized Enterprises and the European Trade Union Confederation. The SBA is a policy framework for promoting growth and creating jobs for SMEs in the EU by specifying regulations for the legal and financial systems of SMEs. In accordance with the SBA, the EU and its member countries are making efforts to promote SME policies such as reducing administrative burdens for SMEs, promoting financial access, and improving market access conditions. As it is central to EU SME policy, I would like to take a closer look at the SBA.

The SBA is a policy for the EU and EU member countries to promote SMEs in order to bolster growth and employment in the EU. It aims to create an environment that realizes SME growth potential by supporting financial and human resources for them within the EU. The goal of the SBA is to eliminate the obstacles to growth for SMEs based on the 'Think Small First' policy. A year after the enactment of the SBA, the EU Parliament passed the SBA resolution and assigned more emphasis on willingness for enforcement. In 2011, the European Commission adopted a 'Review of the Small Business Act', which took stock of the progress and advised of available actions to improve its application.

In this regard, SMEs are considered as a centre of job creation and economic growth in the EU and various support policies were established to this end, which is similar to the situation in Korea. In order to further understand this, we will look at the 10 principles the Small Business Act builds to drive the drafting and implementation of policies to benefit SMEs both at member states level and EU.

Principles of the Small Business Act[5]

1. *Create an environment in which entrepreneurs and family businesses can thrive and entrepreneurship is rewarded*
2. *Ensure that honest entrepreneurs who have faced bankruptcy quickly get a second chance*
3. *Design rules according to the "Think Small First" principle*
4. *Make public administrations responsive to SME needs*
5. *Adapt public policy tools to SME needs: facilitate SME participation in public procurement and better use State Aid possibilities for SMEs*
6. *Facilitate SME access to finance and develop a legal and business environment supportive to timely payments in commercial transactions*
7. *Help SMEs to benefit more from the opportunities offered by the Single Market*
8. *Promote the advancement of skills in SMEs and all forms of innovation*
9. *Enable SMEs to turn environmental challenges into opportunities*
10. *Encourage and support SMEs to benefit from the growth of markets*

5) Reprinted from "Think Small First – A "Small Business Act for Europe, by European Commission, retrieved from https://eur-lex.europa.eu/legal-content/EN/TXT/?uri=CELEX:52008DC0394

However, despite numerous statements made by policymakers, European laws are still far from strict in application of these principles. As the act itself has no binding force, it will be no more than a formality without any substantial influence. Thus, SMEs and their representatives should be included in the legislative process of the act to genuinely apply the 'Think Small First' policy at the European and national level.

3. SME support programs

The SME Performance Review is for managing and evaluating the SBA implementation process of the 28 EU member countries. It provides information on the performance of SMEs in EU member countries in addition to other partner countries. *The Green Action Plan (GAP) for SMEs* helps SMEs in the EU benefit from the transition to a green economy. This plan promotes the transformation towards an inclusive green economy that generates growth, creates jobs, and helps reduce poverty through sustainable management of natural capital. *The Regional SME policies* provide a variety of analysis to increase the competitiveness of SMEs at the regional level to create a business-friendly environment and share best practices SME cases, programs, and policy initiatives.

As most SMEs operate with small scale management and have difficulty receiving help from experts in tax and accounting, tax-related problems are some of the most challenging problems encountered by SMEs in the EU. In addition, the importance of domestic and overseas accounting is increasing for both the shareholders and executives of SMEs. It is becoming a very important aspect for SMEs to have an accounting system that can provide necessary information while avoiding excessive administrative burdens. To solve this problem, the 'Taxation and SMEs' program was initiated to study various tax problems that may arise for SMEs and conduct projects to seek improvement plans. Similar to this is 'Accounting for SMEs', which studies financial law applicable to SMEs and conducts various projects to seek improvement in the legislative environment.

There have also been guidelines adopted to prevent tax delinquency and increase competitiveness in order to protect SMEs. The 'Late Payment Directive' allowed for more rigorous measures than previously available to unify the payment period between public agencies to the companies for the first time. Along those same lines, as companies operating their business in the EU are often faced with debt redemption problems, there is a 'Project on enforcement of outstanding claims' that helps raise awareness and solve problems when they arise.

'The European SME Week' is a pan-European campaign that provides useful information to SMEs in Europe and encourages start-ups. There is also a program that encourages entrepreneurship through organizational rewards and 'The European Enterprise Promotion Awards' in which all EU member countries, as well as organizations in each region such as Iceland, Serbia, and

Turkey, can participate.

Second, there are various programs available to help improve the institutional environment. There is a mentoring program for those who initiate start-ups and a women's support program to reduce the start-up gender gap. The principle of retrial, attempting to start another company when a business fails, is also encouraged. In addition, measures are being supported by 28 member countries to promote SME-friendly administrative actions and entrepreneurship culture.

SMEs often lack the necessary resources to undergo complex administrative procedures or to understand and implement a wide range of regulations and laws. An operational method based on the 'only once' rule has been suggested to simplify the administrative procedures of SMEs. It proposes that, in the legislative process, the guidelines should be minimized using easy to understand language and appropriate exceptions should be provided for SMEs and start-ups. Also, there should be a system established to enable each administrative agency to use the information already entered without requiring submission of the same information several times.

Next, the programs that are provided to strengthen the networks between SMEs can be checked. 'Your Europe Business' is designed to improve the networks between EU member countries and strengthen the advantages of a unified market in Europe. It provides practical information such as legal entitlements, obligations, and opportunities to businesses in the EU.

It also provides overall guidelines in areas such as taxation, finance and funding, overseas exportation, human resources, contracts, and business environment.

There is also the 'Enterprise Europe Network, EEN' which is a program that improves market access for SMEs and facilitates partnerships in other countries within the EU and is divided into three major areas. First, it establishes international partnerships by linking with international partners who can help the growth of EU SMEs. Second, it provides expert advice to help SMEs advance into the global market and grow into global companies. Finally, it provides a solution that enables innovative ideas to be implemented into the business and establishes a network of European SMEs to improve market accessibility. Members of the EEN include universities, research centres, technology centres, and chambers of commerce and industry, all of which provide information, exchange, and services for SMEs.

One of the biggest challenges for EU SMEs is the poor financing environment. The European Commission operates a variety of financial programs aimed at strengthening the competitiveness and sustainability of EU SMEs, encouraging entrepreneurship and promoting their establishment and growth. While enterprises of any size or sector can benefit from this support, the program is specifically focused on supporting the SMEs. The programs aid the SMEs in gaining access to funds via local financial institutions. Various types of financial supports are available, including loans, microfinance, and guarantees or equity funding through venture capital funds, business angels, or social investors.

These entities basically determine the exact financing conditions such as the amount, duration, interest rates, and fees. However, lower interest rates, larger financing volumes, or smaller collateral requirements are available with support from the EU. The EIB Group, which consists of the European Investment Bank (EIB) and the European Investment Fund (EIF), handles the implementation of the programs.

'European Fund for Strategic Investments (EFSI)' is one of the financial programs for SMEs and is considered as the first pillar of the Investment Plan for Europe. One of its main objectives is to support SMEs gaining access to finance. Thus, EFSI has a dedicated window for SMEs that offers up to a total of EUR 5.5 billion, which is supplied as either funding resources or guarantee capacity of products funded by the EIF. With the aid of EFSI, equity funding from venture capital or private equity funds is distributed to innovative companies, even if they have a higher risk profile. EFSI enables this aggressive support in coordination with the other EU programs focusing on SMEs. The support exceeds the amount which could have been provided by the EIF or existing EU instruments without the guarantee from EFSI.

The second area, the 'Programme for the Competitiveness of Enterprises and Small and Medium-sized Enterprises; COSME' is a program to create a favourable environment for funding

SMEs, venture start-ups, and overall growth. This program explains that equity facility and loan guarantee facility should be increased to expand accessibility of SMEs for financing. Thus, COSME aims to provide convenience to the financial activities of SMEs such as creation, expansion, or business transfer. As a result, SMEs in EU countries can have easier access to financial aids channelled through local financial institutions.

Finally, there is 'InnovFin - EU Finance for Innovators,' which is another financing program launched by EIB and EIF. It is a joint initiative in cooperation with the European Commission under the Horizon 2020 program for research and innovation. In addition to a number of integrated and complementary financing tools, it provides advisory services offered by the EIB Group. In order to support investments from all sizes of enterprise, it covers the entire value chain of research and innovation.

4. Start-up status of the EU

Recently, as the start-up venture ecosystem has spread rapidly, many terms have been used to refer to companies in the early stages of foundation. So, what is the difference between start-ups, which are developing into a specific culture in recent years, and SMEs?

'Start-up' refers to a small business in the early stages of its beginning. Initially, this meant a start-up company that lacks funding power but has innovative technology and ideas and was located in Silicon Valley. In general, this refers to an Internet technology-based company with both a high risk and high growth potential. The term start-up emerged when the dot-com bubble of the late 1990s created a start-up boom.

Basically, they are similar to SMEs in a larger framework, but differ from SMEs in that they are in a stage prior to attracting large-scale funds. Unlike institutionalized SMEs, start-ups have no government certification. All small start-up companies in the early stages of foundation can be referred to as start-ups. However, as recent entrepreneurial ecosystems have developed, start-ups have increased, which has created a unique culture. As a result, it has surpassed its previously simple lexical use that only measured the size of a company.

Currently, the status of start-ups in the EU is world-class. The number of specialized developers in Europe is about 5 million, surpassing the US. This is because the labour cost of European experts is relatively lower than that of the US. There is also a sense of open mindedness to foreign manpower and start-ups as a whole. As a result, non-European business partners account for a large portion of the total. EU start-ups are competitive in various fields such as software, data analysis, fashion, marketing, advertising, artificial intelligence, AR, VR, ICT, IoT, HCI, Medical, and 5G and are actively promoting technology standardization.

Let's delve into the efforts of the EU to promote start-ups

within the EU. The source of the digital single market (to remove virtual borders, boost digital connectivity, and make it easier for consumers to access cross-border online content) that the EU is seeking is the start-up. This is an essential component for strengthening EU industrial competitiveness.

The European Commission has created the 'Start-up Europe' program to help create jobs in Europe and to support the growth of EU citizens. It helps build networks between start-ups, investors, entrepreneurs, corporate networks, universities and media, and professionals. They undertake efforts to strengthen investment capabilities not only for networks in Europe, but also in Silicon Valley and India.

They make efforts in a variety of ways to lower unemployment in EU member countries and to nurture young start-up entrepreneurs. The European Commission hosting the European Young Innovators Forum is one such example. In 2017, they provided information on start-ups through tours, the 'Start-up road show', in 10 cities in Europe for 8 months. In addition, they established a network of iLINC and ICT researchers and companies, start-ups, and major legal institutions to run mentoring programs. Since young entrepreneurs are the keystone that makes the start-up business environment of the EU dynamic, they make sure to sufficiently support and invest in them.

Many EU member countries are also making their own best efforts to promote start-ups, with France and the UK being top representatives. France enacted a start-up policy called La

French Tech. This policy has been implemented since 2013 and strived to attract not only French companies, but also companies and outstanding individuals from overseas. Thanks to these efforts, Paris has become a start-up hub in Europe, ranking fifth in the European city start-up index.

Number one in the start-up index of European cities is London. The number of developers in London is larger than that of New York. Their language, English, significantly lowered the language barrier when compared to other cities and has played a pivotal role in allowing London to become the centre of European start-up culture. It is also an attractive city with a large market and ample foreign investment. However, due to Brexit, the labour market is expected to change along with the Euro-

European Digital City Index 2016[6)]

Rank	City	Rank	City	Rank	City	Rank	City
1	London	8	Dublin	46	Milan	54	Rome
2	Stockholm	9	Barcelona	47	Ljubljana	55	Turin
3	Amsterdam	10	Vienna	48	Reel	56	Athens
4	Helsinki	11	Munich	49	Vilnius	57	Zagreb
5	Paris	12	Cambridge	50	Sofia	58	Riga
6	Berlin	13	Bristol	51	Krakow	59	Valletta
7	Copenha-gen	14	Madrid	52	Bucharest	60	Nicosia

6) Adapted from European Digital City Index. Retrieved from https://digitalcityindex.eu/city/25

Networked Readiness Index of European countries[7)]

<table>
<tr><th>Rank</th><th>Country</th><th>Rank</th><th>Country</th><th>Rank</th><th>Country</th></tr>
<tr><td>2</td><td>Finland</td><td>23</td><td>Belgium</td><td>45</td><td>Italy</td></tr>
<tr><td>3</td><td>Sweden</td><td>24</td><td>France</td><td>46</td><td>Macedonia</td></tr>
<tr><td>4</td><td>Norway</td><td>25</td><td>Ireland</td><td>47</td><td>Slovakia</td></tr>
<tr><td>6</td><td>Netherlands</td><td>29</td><td>Lithuania</td><td>50</td><td>Hungary</td></tr>
<tr><td>7</td><td>Swiss</td><td>30</td><td>Portugal</td><td>54</td><td>Croatia</td></tr>
<tr><td>8</td><td>England</td><td>32</td><td>Latvia</td><td>66</td><td>Romania</td></tr>
<tr><td>9</td><td>Luxembourg</td><td>34</td><td>Malta</td><td>69</td><td>Bulgaria</td></tr>
<tr><td>11</td><td>Denmark</td><td>35</td><td>Spain</td><td>70</td><td>Greece</td></tr>
<tr><td>15</td><td>Germany</td><td>36</td><td>Czech Republic</td><td>75</td><td>Serbia</td></tr>
<tr><td>16</td><td>Iceland</td><td>37</td><td>Slovenia</td><td>84</td><td>Albania</td></tr>
<tr><td>20</td><td>Austria</td><td>40</td><td>Cyprus</td><td rowspan="2">97</td><td rowspan="2">Bosnia and Herzegovina</td></tr>
<tr><td>22</td><td>Estonia</td><td>42</td><td>Poland</td></tr>
</table>

pean start-up ecosystem and capital industry. The table below summarizes the start-up index of European cities by dividing them into upper and lower.

The start-up index of European cities and the 'Networked Readiness Index' of all European member countries may show some interesting points. The standard for judging the NRI is accessibility of capital, business environment, digital infrastruc-

7) Adapted from Networked Readiness Index. Retrieved from http://reports.weforum.org/global-information-technology-report-2016/networked-readiness-index/

ture, SME culture, knowledge dissemination, lifestyle, market, mentoring and management support, and non-digital infrastructure. The NRI index is proportional to the income level of member countries. The NRI index is highest mainly in Western and Northern European countries. In comparison, it also shows that the Middle East and Southern Europe have very low digitization capacities.

III. SMEs in Korea

1. Korean SME policies

The number '9988' is mentioned frequently when talking about Korean SMEs. This is the number that represents Korean SMEs and means that the number of SMEs accounts for 99% of the total enterprises and 88% of the total employment. According to these statistics, the SME ratios are similar to that of the EU and about 20% higher in terms of employment. Like the EU, Korea has emphasized that SMEs are the foundation of the economy. In this chapter, we will look at how Korean SME policies have changed over time and examine the characteristics and problems of SMEs in Korea. Lastly, we will compare SME policies between Korea and the EU.

The following table summarizes the changing process of SME policies in Korea and important issues by year.

History of SME policies of Korea[8]

Period	Year	Contents
1945~1960		South Korean SMEs Policies; Establishment of the SME Department in the Ministry of Commerce and Industry
1961~1971	1961	Promulgation of the Law of SME Business 1961-1971-Adjustment; Establishment of the SME Bank
	1962	Establishment of the Korea Federation of Small and Medium Business The Export Promotion Act
	1966	The SME Framework Act Establishment of export industrial complex (Seoul and Incheon)
1972~1981	1974	The Law of Credit Guarantee Fund
	1975	The Law for the Promotion of SME Systematization
	1978	The Law of SME Promotion; Establishment of Small Business Corporation
1982~1992	1982	The Law for the Promotion of Procurement from SMEs (Collective Negotiated Contract System, etc.); Implementing the "SME-Only" Business Policy
	1986	The Law of the Support for SME Start-ups
	1989	The Law of Technology Credit Guarantee Fund; The Law for the Promotion of SMEs and the Procurement of SME Products
1993~1997	1996	Abolition of "SME Only" Policies; Re-structuring and reforming SMEs (Concentrating on technology development, automation of production lines, promotion of Venture) Expanding Obligatory Loans to SME to 45%; Regional SME development Establishment a SME control tower, the Small and Medium Business Administration

8) T Majoni, J Matunhu, and B Chaderopa, "Smes Policies and Challenges: A Comparative Analysis of Zimbabwe and South Korea," *International Journal of Scientific and Research Publications* 6, no. 6 (2016): 381-82.

Period	Year	Contents
1998~2008	1997	The Law of Special Measures for the Promotion of Venture Businesses Amendment on the Small Business Act
	1999	The Law of Women Owned Businesses
2008~Present		The increasing magnitude of bi-lateral and regional free trade regimes - Increasing regulations derived from the augmented awareness on environmental protection - threats and opportunities (e.g. the rise of the green economy, green technology, the" silver" economy) - Generation changes occurring in Korean enterprises

After the Korean War in 1945, Korea focused on post-war reconstruction in the 1950s. Since this was when the national economy was established, there were no separate policies for SMEs. In the 1960s, a legal system began to be established for supporting and fostering SMEs. In 1966, the SME Act was established, and SME policy was introduced. As SMEs were regarded as economically weak from the 1970s to the 1980s, the focus was either on supporting technology development funds or supplying insufficient internal resources. This is because it was necessary to promote SMEs as parts suppliers and producers as the heavy chemical industry policy was being promoted in earnest. Since the launch of the WTO in 1995, Korea has shifted beyond the domestic market to compete in the global market.

Finally, an autonomous and open market was created. Following this, the structure of SMEs in the 1990s began to become more sophisticated. As the interest in technological innovation increased after the financial crisis in 1997, SMEs were regarded as targets for technological innovation. There was a 'venture' at the centre. Venture companies and venture capital were expanded, and the government funded technology development.

Centring on venture policy, measures to compensate for vulnerable sectors such as small businesses were established. The Small Business Act and the Law of Women Owned Businesses were established at this time. Since the 2000s, SMEs have come to lead technological innovation and efforts are made to promote competitive SMEs that can become independent in the global market. In addition to securing proprietary technology, the Act also supports the building of external networks and collaboration with the global market.

2. Status of Korean SMEs

Korean SME standards are applied to both for-profit companies and non-profit organizations, and both size and management independence criteria should be met in order to be considered a SME. In addition, sales and total assets must meet the following standard according to the business type and upper limit criteria. Regardless of the business type, total assets must be less than KRW 500 billion to be classified as a SME.

SME standard in Korea[9]

The main business type of the company	Classification code	Scale
1. Manufacture of apparel, clothing accessories, and fur products	C14	Average sales less than KRW 150 billion
2. Manufacture of leather, bags, and footwear	C15	
3. Manufacture of pulp, paper, and paper products	C17	
4. Manufacture of primary metals	C24	
5. Electrical equipment manufacturing	C28	
6. Furniture manufacturing	C32	
7. Agriculture, forestry, and fisheries	A	Average sales less than KRW 100 billion
8. Mining	B	
9. Food production	C10	
10. Tobacco industry	C12	
11. Textile product manufacturing	C13	
12. Manufacture of Wood and Wood Products	C16	
13. Manufacture of coke, briquette, and refined petroleum products	C19	
14. Chemical and chemical products manufacturing	C20	
15. Manufacture of rubber products and plastic products	C22	
16. Manufacture of metal processing products	C25	

9) *Republic of Korea: Enforcement Decree of the Framework Act on Small and Medium Enterprises*. Article 2 and Presidential Decree No. 29552, Feb. 14, 2019.

The main business type of the company	Classification code	Scale
17. Manufacture of electronic components, computers, video, sound, and communication equipment	C26	Average sales less than KRW 100 billion
18. Other machinery and equipment manufacturing	C29	
19. Automobile and trailer manufacturing	C30	
20. Other transportation equipment manufacturing	C31	
21. Other transportation equipment manufacturing	D	
22. Water service	E36	
23. Construction industry	F	
24. Wholesale and Retail	G	
25. Beverage manufacturing	C11	Average sales less than KRW 80 billion
26. Printing and recording media duplication business	C18	
27. Manufacture of medical materials and pharmaceuticals	C21	
28. Manufacture of non-metallic mineral products	C23	
29. Medical, precision, optics and watch manufacturing	C27	
30. Other products manufacturing	C33	
31. Water, sewage, and waste disposal, raw material recycling	E	
32. Transportation and Warehousing	H	
33. Information and communication industry	J	

The main business type of the company	Classification code	Scale
34. Repair of industrial machinery and equipment	C34	Average sales less than KRW 60 billion
35. Professional, scientific, and technical services	M	
36. Business facilities management, business support and rental services	N	
37. Health and social welfare services	Q	
38. Arts, sports, and leisure services	R	
39. Repair and other personal services	S	

When the standard for the scope of SMEs in Korea is set by the number of employees in the company, it's shown as follows. Korea has changed the standards of SMEs in response to rapid economic growth.

The scope of SMEs in Korea[10]

	Basic law '93.3.6		Enforcement decree '95.7.1,' 96.3.28		Enforcement decree '97.12.27,' 98.2.28	
	Applied in 1994		Applied from 1995~1996		Applied from 1997~2000	
	SME	Medium	SME	Medium	SME	Medium
Manufacturing	≤20	21~300	≤50	51~300	≤50	51~300
Transportation	≤20	21~300	≤50	51~300	≤50	51~300
Construction	≤20	21~200	≤30	31~200	≤30	31~200
Wholesale, retail, and other services	≤5	6~20	≤10	11~20	≤10	11~20

10) Ibid.

In 2015, Korean SMEs accounted for 99.89% of the total number of businesses, which is 0.02% lower than 2014. However, in the 2000s, the number of SMEs has been on an increasing trend.

Number of Enterprises in Korea[11]

(Unit: company, %)

	2015			2014			2013		
	Total	SME	Large	Total	SME	Large	Total	SME	Large
Enter-prises	3,604,773	3,600,882	3,891	3,545473	3,542,350	3,123	3,418,993	3,415,863	3,130
Ratio	100.00	99.89	0.11	100.00	99.91	0.09	100.00	99.91	0.09

Number of Employees of SMEs in Korea[12]

(Unit: company, %)

	2015			2014			2013		
	Total	SME	Large	Total	SME	Large	Total	SME	Large
Employ-ees	16,774,98	15,127,047	1,647,901	15,962,745	14,027,636	1,985,109	15,344,860	13,421,594	1,923,266
Ratio	100.00	90.18	9.82	100.00	87.88	12.12	100.00	87.47	12.53

In 2015, the number of employees in Korean SMEs accounted for 90.18%, which is 2.3% higher than 2014, and it has been confirmed that the number employees in SMEs is increasing every year. This shows a similar rate compared to that of the

11) Ministry of SMEs and Startups. *Statistics of Korean SMEs*, retrieved from https://www.mss.go.kr/site/eng/02/10204000000002016111504.jsp
12) Ibid.

EU. However, the productivity gap between SMEs and large enterprises is larger in Korea. The figure below shows the employment share of SMEs and the wage gap (Large enterprise wage=100) between SMEs and larger enterprises by year since 1985.

Proportion of SME employment and changes in relative wages (1985~2013)[13]

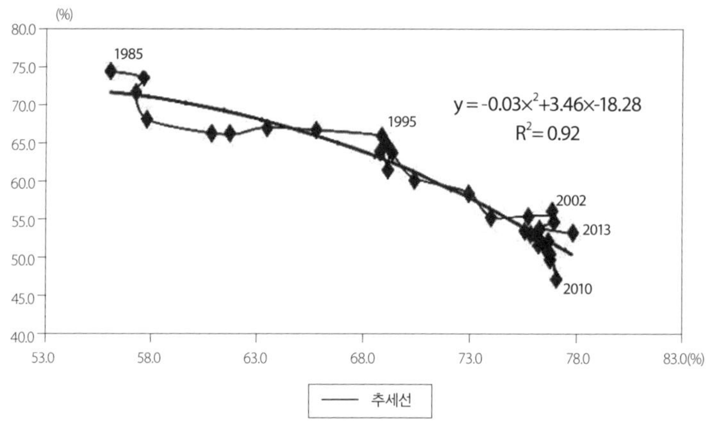

This confirms that the proportion of SME employment has increased as the wage gap between SMEs and large enterprises has widened. Over a long period of time from 1985 to 2013, the wage gap between large enterprises and SMEs continued to expand from 74.5% to 53.2%, while the proportion of SME employment has increased steadily from 56.1% to 77.9%. In other words, the employment of SMEs in Korea has increased by absorbing low-

13) Deok-Hee Cho, "Reinterpretation of the meaning and implications SMEs 9988, *Korea Institute for Industrial Economics & Trade Issue Paper* (2016): 43.

wage employment while increasing the wage gap between large enterprises and SMEs. Also, the number of micro-sized SMEs has increased significantly.

Starting from a few years ago, the problem of identifying the number of SME employees has been raised. Some point out that the Korean government does not examine the status of SMEs precisely, which may lead to implementation of incorrect policies. The employment statistics from the National Statistical Office are from a corporate unit survey based on administrative data. The proportion of SME employees is lower than the stated 90.18% due to the fact that the corporate unit survey considers the head office and branches as a single company. According to the employment statistics, the proportion of SME employees was 80.4% in 2015 and 80.8% in 2016 in for-profit companies. This shows a significant difference from the results of the business unit survey which showed 88~90%. Taking into account employment for both for-profit and non-profit (public sector like government, schools, hospitals, etc.) companies, the share of employees in companies with 300 or more employees accounted for 27.8% in 2016.

The proportion of employees in companies with less than 300 employees (SME classification criteria by 2014) is 72.2%. The '9988' number is a statistical paradigm claimed by the Korean government leading to a widespread perception that 'the share of SME employees is 88%'. However, the reality is about 80%, and when combined with non-profit companies such as government, schools, and hospitals, it falls to 72%. If we look at the proportion of SME employees with this gap, the vision for SME policies will change accordingly. Overestimating the number of SMEs and the proportion of SME employees may lead to excessive SME policies, which refers to excessive support of SMEs. It also results in underestimating the role of large enterprises.

3. Start-up status in Korea

With the rapid progress of the fourth industrial revolution, start-ups based on new ideas and technologies are growing at a rapid pace. The main examples are Xiaomi, Uber, and Palantir which have been leading the global ICT industry since their establishment. In particular, interest in the start-up ecosystem has increased since the global financial crisis in 2009.

One of the survival strategies for the long-term global recession is support for the establishment of the start-up ecosystem. In response to this trend, the importance of the start-up ecosystem is being emphasized even more in Korea. Here, the research will delve into the status of the Korean start-up market and support programs from the government. The goal is to discover implications for the establishment of a Korean start-up ecosystem by comparing it with the European case mentioned earlier.

New venture capital investment in start-ups has reached record highs for three consecutive years. According to the Korea Venture Capital Association, new venture capital investment in

2016 recorded KRW 2.1503 trillion, exceeding the record high of KRW 2.0858 trillion, in 2015. This implies that domestic venture capital firms are maintaining their steady investment in start-ups despite the doubt in the global market regarding their growth potential. New venture funds, which crossed the KRW 3 trillion mark for the first time, are at KRW 3.1998 trillion. This is a 17.9% increase compared to the previous year.

Amount of New VC Investment in Korea by year[14)]

(Unit: KRW, 100 million)

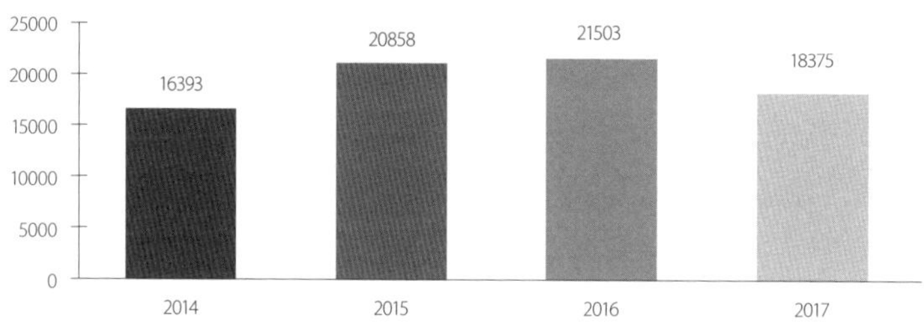

However, the corporate value of start-ups in Korea is still low despite this growth. As of February 2019, there were only six unicorn companies in Korea. A unicorn company refers to an unlisted start-up that has a corporate value of over USD 1 billion. A unicorn is a legendary horse with a horn on its head. This term was coined by the female venture investor Aileen Lee. What this means is that there are a lot of start-ups, but they are

---

14) Adapted from VC Statistics. Retrieved from http://www.kvca.or.kr/en/Program/vc_statistics/list.html?a_gb=eng&a_cd=3&a_item=0&sm=4_2

rarely successful like the imaginary unicorn. Subsequently, the number of unicorn companies is the standard of success of a nation's start-up ecosystem and an indicator of the fourth industrial revolution. Since 2014, many unicorn companies have emerged in the global market and their establishment rate has been accelerated since 2017. In 2019, the total number of global unicorn companies is 310, that is, 110 new companies were added compared to last year, which is a 55% increase.

Korean Unicorn Start-ups Valued at USD 1B+ (AS OF 1/23/19)[15]

Company	Valuation(USD M)	Category
Bluehole	USD 5,000	Internet Software & Services
Coupang	USD 9,000	E-commerce
L&P Cosmetic	USD 1,780	Other
Viva Republica (Toss)	USD 1,200	Fintech
Woowa Brothers (Baedal Minjok)	USD 2,600	E-commerce
Yello Mobile	USD 4,000	Other

According to the Korean start-up ecosystem forum white paper, which surveyed 295 start-up companies in Seoul and Seongnam, 116 of 295 companies were established after 2015. By industry, ICT services are number 1. A major characteristic of

15) Adapted from The Global Unicorn Club. Retrieved from https://www.cbinsights.com/research-unicorn-companies

Korean start-ups is that more investing occurs in the later stages than in the initial stages of investment. This is contrary to that of the global market. In addition, the capital is often less than KRW 100 million at the time of establishment, which is considered very small, and more than half of the companies still have capital of less than KRW 100 million when compared to the time of establishment. According to a survey of funding sources at the time of establishment, personal funds are the highest at 19.9% and this was mainly from technology guarantee funding, government funding, and angel investment/accelerators, whereas venture capital investment was only 8.3%. Also, 53.9% did not receive any external investment.

According to the Venture Capital Market Brief by the Korean Venture Capital Association, half of the new funding sources for venture companies in Korea are government policy funds. Despite the increase in venture capital investment, new venture funding through venture capital and angel investment is still insufficient. M&A and IPO are the main methods for investors to collect funds. M&A is common in the investment collection of major countries such as the USA and Israel, while in Korea, Initial Public Offerings (IPO) are relatively high. The domestic M&A collection rate is only 1~2%, which is a negative factor for investment expansion, such as venture capital.

According to the 2018 Survey of Korea Venture Firms, the greatest challenge in managing a start-up business was 'difficulties in managing funds such as funding and operation' at 74.6%, followed by 'securing and maintaining necessary manpower' at 54.9%, 'commercialization of developed technologies' at 54.9%, and 'pioneering the market' at 51.8%. Although the government has proposed various policies to increase the number of domestic start-up unicorn companies to 10 by 2023, many companies do not receive any practical assistance regardless of these efforts.

IV. Final Remark: Possible Changes and Challenges in the policy of SME and Start-up

According to the case of the EU mentioned earlier, we have found that governments, businesses, and academics from 28 countries in the EU actively support start-ups and investments in establishing a SME and start-up friendly ecosystem. The Korean government needs to clarify the basic roles of SMEs and start-up support policies to better strategically focus on. Strengthening competitiveness should be the priority. An increase in the employment of SMEs without innovation shall lead to a decline in competitiveness. It is important to link policy objectives with measures. In addition, we should focus on practical technical support rather than considering SMEs and start-ups as a social weaknesses needing protection.

It is also time to re-verify the start-up environment and perceptions. The Korean government considers start-ups to be a new breakthrough in the era of low-growth, supports many start-ups, and encourages young entrepreneurship in particular. However, according to the 'study on the perception of start-ups in Korea, China and Japan' by the Korea International Trade Association, it shows that Korean students are considering starting a business as an alternative to employment. In addition, the top desired start-up business was restaurant, which implies that it is focused on living and low value-added business start-ups. This is different from the global market, where technology-based start-ups are expanding more rapidly.

The EU is paying attention to young people in each member country to create a foundation for growth through start-ups, to stimulate and innovate existing businesses, and to contribute to job creation. In particular, a foundation for long-term development of start-ups has been established as there is a view that substantial innovation and job creation occurs when start-ups expand their scale.

From this point of view, European countries are establishing a growth foundation for start-ups centered on industrial clusters. In addition, they create a 'win-win' partnership by linking start-ups with large companies that have globalization capabilities centered on those clusters.

We should pay attention to the fact that the European start-up eco system ultimately aims at promoting globalization of start-ups from the initial stages. As the proportion of global customers in Korean start-ups (14%) is much lower than the global average of 23% (Start-up Genome), we can learn much from Europe.

Another issue that Korean start-ups and SMEs have to solve is 'regulation'. According to the Internal Market Burdens or Entry Regulation by Global Entrepreneurship Monitor (GEM), Korea ranked 49th out of 65 countries (as of 2016), which indicates a poor start-up environment. It is impressive that Note that nine of the top 10 countries are members of the EU. It is urgent to benchmark the cases of these countries to improve the start-up environment in Korea.

In addition, in the 'Product Market Regulation', which is related to entry regulations in the PMR indicator announced by the OECD, Korea is in 29th place (as of 2013) among 35 countries, which demonstrates the difficulty of new entries into the market. In addition, from 1998 to 2013, Korea has remained at the lowest rank among the OECD countries for 15 years. This confirms that the 'entry regulation' has not been improved.

The following table summarizes the businesses that cannot even be started in Korea because of regulations. The EU, the US and China are removing or reducing regulations for new businesses to develop leading-edge technologies. Compared to those countries, Korea is still lagging behind in innovation due to regulations.

Internal Market Burdens or Entry Regulation[16]

(Weighted average: 1 = highly insufficient, 9 = highly sufficient)

Rank	Country	Value
1	Netherlands	6.2
2	Estonia	5.6
3	Austria	5.4
4	Luxembourg	5.4
5	Switzerland	5.3
6	Germany	5.2
7	Georgia	5.1
8	UK	5.1
9	Finland	5.0
10	Australia	5.0
11	India	5.0
15	US	4.7
22	China	4.4
49	Korea	3.8

The systematic and changing strategies of the EU have great implications for Korea, which is held back by regulations. We should be aware of the fact that the Korean government's tight regulation becomes a huge barrier to new technology develop-

16) Niels Bosma and Donna Kelley, "Global Entrepreneurship Monitor. *2018/2019 Global Report. Gráfica Andes, Chile* (2018).

ment and business. The exemplary cases of the EU should be referred to and existing regulations should be readjusted to take into account new industry trends. The government should play a leading role in creating agreement through ongoing discussions, coordination, and consultation with existing business people.

List of Global Unicorn companies and their legal hurdles in Korea[17]

Company	Business contents	Legal hurdles in Korea
Uber, Lyft, Grab	Car sharing	Passenger transport service act
GuaHao (WeDoctor), Proteus Digital Health	Remote Medical care	Medical law
23andMe	Private genetic testing	Bioethics Law
Ehang	Drone Taxi	Aviation Safety Act, Aviation Business Act

The main implication we can surmise through the EU support program for SMEs is that the EU considers economic growth through SMEs to be a top priority. In addition, they strive to develop the regional economy in a balanced manner through the division of roles between large enterprises and SMEs.

17) Adapted from The Global Unicorn Club. Retrieved from https://www.cbinsights.com/research-unicorn-companies

Chapter 4.
Reconciliation in Europe and Northeast Asia: Korean-Japanese and German-Polish Relations after World War II

Reconciliation in Europe and Northeast Asia: Korean-Japanese and German-Polish Relations after World War II

Ewa Motylińska

I. Introduction

In the aftermath of gruesome conflicts, some former adversary countries managed to establish long-lasting peace whereas others could not achieve even a partial reconciliation. What is the role of historical memory in shaping post-conflict interstate relationships and does history education really matter in the process of popular reconciliation?

The twentieth century was vastly marked by violent and bloody conflicts, after which struggles for the restoration of mutual trust and peace started. The problem of successful strategy for post conflict interstate reconciliation was repeatedly addressed on both a political and an academic level. The significance of successful reconciliation strategy is illuminated by post-Cold War order. When the Iron Curtain collapsed, bitterness about historical wrongdoings emerged again.

While Northeast Asia has witnessed growth in regional interactions over the last twenty years, especially in the areas of culture and economy, scars from past wrongs, committed during colonialism and war, have remained. The question of history has become a highly contentious diplomatic issue and a centerpiece in national identity, crowding out other dimensions and complicating bilateral relations. On the other hand, after the fall of communism, Poland and the reunited Germany have had a mostly positive but occasionally strained relationship due to some political issues. After the collapse of the USSR, Germany has been a proponent of Poland's participation in NATO and the EU.

This chapter argues that the historical memory and national identity matter in post-conflict interstate relations and that the key to realizing deep interstate reconciliation is to understand the position of the other party and a harmonization of an interpretation of common history. The national history discrepancies that result from national mythmaking can significantly obstruct the long-term reconciliation process. For the purpose, this research examines two post-World War II cases: Polish-German and Korean-Japanese relations. These two cases are similar in their geographical proximity, cultural and economic ties, and experience of traumatic conflict. At the same time, the process and finally the outcome of reconciliation differs significantly.

To study the different aspects of deep reconciliation, mainly two theories are considered. The first is a realist theory that considers states to be the principal actors in the international relations, concerned only with their own national interest and security.[1] Proponents of realist theory assume that cooperation among states is a rare phenomenon and only those with the common external threat would develop cooperation. When governments decide to maintain cooperation, public feelings and popular relations should also be friendly, because for realists, states are the only unitary actors. Thus, deep reconciliation exists, but it is conditioned by current distribution and balance of power in the international system. According to this theory "memories and myths are epiphenomenal, changing in accordance with the external environment: If posing a mutual threat, states will demonize one another and grow mutual hatred; if a common threat arises, they will forget the past, discard hatred, and develop cooperation".[2]

The second is national mythmaking theory, which considers domestic politics and historical memory placed in societal context as important factors shaping interstate relations. The national mythmaking theory suggests that elite mythmaking of the traumatic post-conflict history for their own purposes can hinder deep reconciliation. The practice of creating myths is

1) Julian W. Korab-Karpowicz, "Political Realism in International Relations," *The Stanford Encyclopedia of Philosophy* 2013.
2) Yinan He, *The Search for Reconciliation. Sino-Japanese and German-Polish Relations since World War II* (New York: Cambridge University Press, 2009).

very common in political and social life. Thus, national mythmaking theory asks two questions: "Why and how are myths of traumatic history made?" and "how does mythmaking affect interstate reconciliation outcomes?" . This study considers mainly the second question with outlining the first one. According to this theory, the ruling elites, pursuing particular political and ideological goals, tend to create myths that glorify or whitewash the history of its own nation, especially this concerning past conflicts, while exaggerating actions of the other party. Such myths, prevalent in national consciousness, cause sharp disagreement between two former hostile states on the interpretation of their common past. By such disagreements, both elites and the general public will develop not only mistrust against each other's country but also emotions of grievances and frustration, causing even more negative stereotypes within society. Moreover, public resentments over the historical issues obstruct governments from conciliatory policies in other areas. On the contrary, states which agree on the basic common interpretation of their conflict history and take prompt measures to compensate the past wrongdoings are more likely to deal with the post-conflict trauma, grievances among people and by this facilitating reconciliation also on intergovernmental level.

To evaluate the two theories, comparative case study was used as the primary methodology. Spatial scope is targeted to two dyads in Europe and Asia; Germany-Poland and Korea-Japan. The two cases are similar in many dimensions such as geographical proximity, economic and cultural relations, and memories of traumatic war. Despite many similarities, both the process of reconciliation and the outcome differ significantly. In a short time, the united Germany and Poland, have successfully dealt with the painful past and achieved meaningful reconciliation, whereas the relationship between Korea and Japan is still marked by mistrust and animosity. Thus, the two dyads seem to be adequate for comparing why and how the degree of interstate reconciliation varies across cases.

The analysis of case studies has been conducted mainly based on the process tracing and congruence procedure. Applied congruence tests rely on cross-case and within-case comparison. The German-Polish and Korean-Japanese dyads have large within-case variance in both independent and dependent variables. This allows the causal argument to be tested repeatedly over time with just two cases, as both dyads provide sufficient number of different units of analysis in such a great length of time.

When testing the realist and national mythmaking theory against each subcase, the study investigates whether the values in the dependent and independent variables covary and confirm the predications of the respective theories.

II. Explaining Interstate Reconciliation

Prior to present in detail different theoretical approaches toward interstate reconciliation, this chapter defines genuine reconciliation as the concept of Deep Interstate Reconciliation (DIR), where countries share the understanding that war is unthinkable and hold generally warm feelings toward each other. This concept has been broadly introduced by He in her book "The Search for Reconciliation" (2009). According to it, "DIR needs to be cemented not only by shared short-run material interests but also by sustainable mutual understanding and trust". This chapter introduces the conceptual framework of deep interstate reconciliation and develops an operational definition of the term.

1. Conceptualizing Deep Interstate Reconciliation

Although there are a number of different statements defining reconciliation, the general idea of reconciliation in this study is understood as "restoring friendly relationships, harmony, and communication" between two parties, which experienced trauma in the past.[3] International relations usually associate the traumatic experience with an aftermath of destructive conflicts. Such conflicts not only cause enormous casualties, and a violation of basic human rights, but can also lead to loss of territory,

---

3) Ann L Phillips, "The Politics of Reconciliation: Germany in Central East Europe," *German Politics* 7, no. 2 (1998).

or even national annexation. Alongside with suffering caused by physical damages, states and individuals often experience humiliation. Such historical occurrences create deep-rooted collective sorrow and grief[4] that eventually turns into national trauma, making former enemies prone to mutual hatred.[5] The interstate reconciliation is mainly about overcoming this enmity arising from past traumatic events.

The conceptual framework for understanding deep interstate reconciliation should contain two key components - stable peace and amicable atmosphere - that cover both intergovernmental and people-to-people relationships. Deep interstate reconciliation means that former adversaries reached a high degree of peacefulness and they are not prone to fight again. History gives some examples of cases in which despite the absence of open conflict, there is hard to talk about peaceful relationships. In other words, even in the absence of war per se, in such cases relations between entities can still be precarious and might easily deteriorate into armed conflict. The so-called long peace during the Cold War was interrupted by international crises and proxy wars. What is more, even the stability of the US and the USSR has been constantly questioned.

As Thomas Hobbes pointed out in his remarkable work *Leviathan*, "War consists not in battle only, or the act of fighting,

---

4) Elazar Barkan, *The Guilt of Nations: Restitution and Negotiating Historical Injustices* (JHU Press, 2001), 345.
5) Ibid.

but in a tract of time, wherein the will to contend by battle is sufficiently known: and therefore the notion of time is to be considered in the nature of war, as it is in the nature of weather. For as the nature of foul weather lies not in a shower or two of rain, but in an inclination thereto of many days together: so, the nature of war consists not in actual fighting, but in the known disposition thereto during all the time there is no assurance to the contrary. All other time is peace."[6]

Therefore, it is impossible to define deep reconciliation in terms of "no war". In order to define and characterize the concept of deep interstate reconciliation, Boulding's interpretation of stable peace can be used, which is the "situation in which probability of war is so small that it does not really enter into the calculations of any of the people involved."[7] What he also suggests is the fact that stable peace is not only about avoiding conflicts but also about how those conflicts are handled. In other words, this concept convinces that war is an unthinkable way of resolving international conflict.

In a process of reconciliation building, stable peace is essential but not the only element. In addition to stable peace on official, state-to-state level, deep reconciliation needs an amicable atmosphere on people-to-people level. As Willy Brandt (1978) said, "Reconciliation cannot be decreed by politicians must mature

---

6) Kenneth E. Boulding, *Stable Peace* (Austin: University of Texas Press, 1978).

7) He, *The Search for Reconciliation. Sino-Japanese and German-Polish Relations since World War II.*

in the hearts of people on both sides." Without a good will of the people, deep interstate reconciliation is replaced by fragile armistice.

For nations that have experienced post-war trauma, harmony is only possible to reach, when deeply rooted people-to-people animosity has been naturalized.[8] It does not mean that the traumatic collective memory will be removed from social discourse, but when new interstate dispute arises, tendency of using history as an argument will be decreasing. When such a state will be attained, the relationships between the peoples from former hostile countries will be characterized by mutual trust and amiability.

2. An Operational Definition of Interstate Reconciliation

According to Boulding's theory, international war-peace system consists of four general phases: stable war, unstable war, unstable peace, and stable peace. The system shifts from one phase to another, whenever the stability of the system is questionable. Regarding this definition, post conflict reconciliation can be seen as a systematic transition from the stage of unstable peace, which is characterized by possible recurrence of conflict, to the stage of stable peace, in which the threat of war is close to nonexistence.[9]

---

8) Ibid
9) He, *The Search for Reconciliation. Sino-Japanese and German-Polish*

Boulding also defines three steps of reconciliation: nonreconciliation, shallow reconciliation, and deep reconciliation. Each step can be understood in terms of an intergovernmental dimension, as well as, in a people-to-people dimension. Following the strategy introduced by He in her book *The Search for Reconciliation*, three indicators can be used to measure intergovernmental relationships: (1) mutual expectation of war, (2) national recognition, and (3) economic interaction. Indicator number one is the most important since it defines state of stable peace. The other two indicators are useful in depicting deviations in other aspects of intergovernmental relationships. As the indicator assessing people-to-people dimension of reconciliation, the degree of mutual trust can be used as measured by the public opinion survey, as well as academic studies on bilateral popular relationships.[10)]

Table 1 shows the typology of the various stages of interstate reconciliation. Nonreconciliation means a state of affairs characterized by mutual hatred and fear among the nations in post-conflict countries. It includes 'imminent expectations of war', 'minimal economic interaction' and lack of 'national recognition' between the governments of the states. The next stage is 'shallow reconciliation', which can be presented in two variants: either 'friction' or 'rapprochement'. The outcome of shallow

Relations since World War II.

10) Alastair I Johnston, *The Correlates of Nationalism in Beijing Public Opinion, 1998-2002* (S. Rajaratnam School of International Studies, 2003).

Table 1. *Measuring Interstate Reconciliation*[11)]

	Nonreconciliation	Shallow Reconciliation		Deep Reconciliation
		Friction	Rapprochement	
Government-to-government	Imminent expectation of war	Moderate expectation of war: *Prepare for remote war*	Moderate expectation of war: *Cautious cooperation*	Shared expectation of no war
	No national recognition	Partial national recognition: *Sovereignty disputes politicized*	Partial national recognition: Sovereignty disputes Deferred	Full national recognition
	Minimal economic Interaction	Limited economic interaction: *Economic friction Politicized*	Limited economic inter action: *Economic friction subdued*	Comprehensive and smooth economic interaction
People-to-people	Popular hatred and fear	Moderate popular tension: *Estrangement and suspicion*	Moderate popular tension: *Illusory friendship possible*	Harmonious mutual feeling

11) Adapted from: He, *The Search for Reconciliation. Sino-Japanese and German-Polish Relations since World War II.*

reconciliation is so-called popular tension characterized either by 'estrangement and suspicion' (friction) or through 'illusory friendship' (rapprochement). In such case, moderate expectations of war would be perceived in two ways, either as "cautious cooperation' (rapprochement) or 'preparation for remote war' (friction).

National recognition would not be fully accomplished, and economic interaction would be limited, with trade friction politicized or subdued. At the very end of reconciliation process there is a deep reconciliation, characterized by mutual harmony between governments, as well as, the people of respective countries.[12] Other necessary conditions for this stage are: 'common expectation of no war' between the governments; 'comprehensive and smooths economic interaction'; and 'full national recognition', which means that both governments have not only recognized one another's legal status but at the same time resolved all territorial and jurisdictional disputes.[13]

3. The Realist Theory on Interstate Reconciliation

Realism is a broad theoretical paradigm, which includes many different variants and combinations. To broadly explains the formation and specific characteristics of various types of post conflict interstate relations, this study focuses mainly on the

---

12) Allen Carlson, *Unifying China, Integrating with the World: Securing Chinese Sovereignty in the Reform Era* (NUS Press, 2008), 11-15.

13) Boulding, *Stable Peace*.

branch dealing with external material threats.[14] Realists perceive post-war interstate reconciliation in terms of international political cooperation. From the realist perspective such cooperation is difficult because in a world mired in anarchy every state focuses on maximizing its own power to survive and prosper. The pressure of being self-sufficient leads to increased competition between states.[15]

Anarchy requires states to worry about the relative gains of cooperation and the possibility that adversaries will cheat on agreements.[16] Therefore, states are more likely to collaborate when countering a common threat. When states, by helping each other, enforce defence against a common external enemy, concerns about relative gains of the allies are less important. Thus, neorealists argue that structural conditions have the most significant impact on one's decision whether to cooperate with another state. Generally, this realist theory makes two predictions regarding post conflict intergovernmental relations. According to the first one, the bigger common threats states face, the likelihood of intergovernmental reconciliation is higher. Conversely, the stronger the mutual threat and mistrust is, the lover is the likelihood of reaching reconciliation.

The theory also predicts three different outcomes according

---

14) Ibid.
15) Kenneth N. Waltz, *Theory of International Politics* (MA: Addison-Wesley, 1979), 105-07.
16) Charles L. Glaser, "Realists as Optimists: Cooperation as Self-Help," *International Security* (1994/95).

to the intensity of the relations.[17] Firstly, states facing a serious common security threat are more likely to accomplish official reconciliation in order to become stronger. Bilateral relations would be characterized by absolute gains concerns, which should accelerate the process of political reconciliation, as well as, economic cooperation. The second possible outcome occurs when states pose a mutual threat, when engaging in strategic rivalry. A similar situation occurs, when states join rivalling power blocs in search of powerful allies. Under such negative structural conditions, military conflict is likely to occur, whereas economic and political cooperation become almost impossible to pursue. Hence, intergovernmental reconciliation is out of the question. Thirdly, neutral structural conditions appear when the common security threat has decreased, or the states' mutual threat has diminished. When tension between states decrease, they are more likely to start economic, as well as political cooperation. In such a case, intergovernmental reconciliation would be a slow and gradual process with certain limitations.

For realists, nation-states are the only unitary, rational actors in the international relations. Thus, they do not consider attributes of popular relations, such as public opinion or individuals' activities, as significant factors shaping international relations. The only predication regarding popular relations that realists make argues that the greater the structural condition, the great-

17) Ibid.

er the probability that two nations will reconcile.

Additionally, reconciliation at the popular level would be also driven by security concerns rather than genuine feelings of individuals. In such a circumstance, the official policy of both states will facilitate cooperation on societal level in order to use friendship propaganda to enhance sense of companionship between the two nations. As a result, the two nations are not willing to fight, and the two governments can enter the path of reconciliation.[18]

On the contrary, mutual threat will antagonize both nations by generating mistrust and fear among the general public. In such a case, history and post-conflict trauma will be used as a convenient justification for violent confrontation. What is more, official propaganda will effectively discourage if not prohibit people from both countries to cooperate in any respect. Hence, probability of reconciliation will be very small or even equal to zero. In other words, two countries will remain on stage of non-reconciliation.

In the case of neutral structural conditions, when there are no direct mutual or common threats, official policy will facilitate societal contacts with some limitations due to remaining inexplicit security concerns. When popular relations are characterized by partial amicable atmosphere, even insignificant conflict of interest can increase antipathy between two nations. In such

---

18) Korab-Karpowicz, "Political Realism in International Relations."

a circumstance, both sides will be likely to use history as a tool of pressure. When this conflict of interest calms down, history disputes and mutual resentment will be forgotten for a while. Such a state of affairs, together with limited interstate cooperation will place the two countries at the stage of shallow reconciliation.

Using realist theory to address complex set of questions regarding reconciliation may seem irrelevant since it does not focus on popular relations. Nevertheless, there are three reasons to apply this theory. First of all, reconciliation is still an understudied area in terms of international relations. Secondly, the theory of external material threat predicts that deep reconciliation can occur but it does not mean that it has to be a permanent state. Interstate harmony cannot outlast the common security threat faced by states. As long as the security incentives are present, the harmony is likely to last. Thirdly, even though realists rarely consider popular relations as an important subject to study, their thought patterns and way of predicting can be applied. For realists, the only recognized unitary actors on the stage of international relations are states and popular feelings are just an integral part of governmental policy, which follow it whenever international structure transforms. Thus, realist theory considers people-to-people relations in terms of unit-level attribute, which should be placed in the structural context.[19]

---

19) Glaser, "Realists as Optimists: Cooperation as Self-Help."

4. The National Mythmaking Theory on Interstate Reconciliation

National mythmaking theory holds significant explanatory power in understanding the failure of some countries to achieve deep post conflict interstate reconciliation. The main purpose of national mythmaking theory is to explain how historical myth and certain ideas may affect post conflict interstate relations. Moreover, this theory considers ideas and historical myths as 'an independent source of foreign policy'.[20]

This theory is a young theory that draws from many different disciplines such as, history, psychology, political and social science. The core idea of the theory is that 'memory is an image of the past collectively constructed by members of a social group in the present'.[21] One of the problems related to national memory is the fact that ruling elites often create or use already existing national myths for their own purposes and try to install them into collective memory within a social institutional framework. In such a case, divergent, often self-whitewashing or other-maligning memories adopted in societies of former enemy countries negatively affect not only people-to-people relations but also official intergovernmental relations. According to He, mutual threat perception may become exacerbated at both

20) Stephan R. Rock, *Why Peace Breaks Out: Great Power Reapprochmenr in Historical Perspective* (Chapel Hill: University of North Carolina Press, 1989).
21) Waltz, *Theory of International Politics*.

official and popular levels, through mechanisms of *emotion* and *intention*.

It is worth mentioning that national mythmaking theory is significantly different from manipulation of historical facts performed by ruling groups repeatedly over the centuries. First of all, in accordance with the assumptions of the mythmaking theory, myths must be created within the acceptable limitation of historical context to gain widespread support. Secondly, mythmaking should not be understood in terms of a simply top-down coherent process but as a structure resulting from complex discourse on national memory.[22]

Memories are not only a matter of individuals or small communities, some social variables should be discussed in terms of social or even national memory, which are far beyond individual memory. Such memories created within a framework of social discourse and placed in memorials, museums, and textbooks as time passes turn into elements of collective national memory.

Emile Durkheim noticed that societies require connection with the past to maintain social unity and cohesion. While studying religious traditions, he noted that rituals transmit traditional beliefs, values and rules, which provide a sense of collective consciousness. He suggested that collective thought required individuals to join together physically, in order to create a common experience that would be shared by whole the group.

---

22) Glaser, "Realists as Optimists: Cooperation as Self-Help."

Since the collective thought required the physical gathering, it was essential for groups to develop methods of preserving that unity when the group was disbanded. Durkheim believed that such items as totems held immense power, by which provided individuals with a device transmitting the past to the present.[23]

Maurice Halbwachs suggested that individual memory can be understood only through a group context, since it was constructed within social structures such as families, various organizations, and nation-states. Individuals understand and organize concepts and events within a social context; hence, they remember them in a way that rational order of things requires. Moreover, every collective memory is directly related to particular groups that are delineated by time and space. Halbwachs also adopted an instrumental presentist approach toward collective memory, which states that construction of collective memory is strongly influenced by the present issues. In other words, certain groups choose different memories in order to explain current affairs and concerns. Depending on situation, ruling groups reconstruct and rearrange the past events to fit into the social narrative.[24]

Pierre Nora expanded Halbwachs' instrumental presentism claiming that groups select certain events from the past and invent new traditions to strengthen the collective memory, while

---

23) He, *The Search for Reconciliation. Sino-Japanese and German-Polish Relations since World War II.*

24) Ibid.

deliberately eliminating others, creating collective amnesia. He also noted that in most cases those in power select the representations of collective memory. Hence, collective memory is both an object and a tool of power. What is more Nora suggested that national histories are often manipulated by ruling elites to adjust it according to their present needs and interests.[25]

In contrast to Halbwachs and Nora, He argues that collective memory does not have to be an object of political game. Such groups as family, local community, or gender group can hold their memories based on common values, tradition, and cultural norms far from being instrumental. However, when history becomes a tool in political struggle, the situation dramatically changes.

When ruling elites start to manipulate history, national myths arise. According to Anderson national myths are inspiring narratives or fanciful stories about a nation's past, origin, or identity.[26] Such myths significantly influence national values and often serve as important national symbols. The fact that they might not precisely represent historical events does not reduce their power. As Christensen argues,[27] ruling elites may deliberately construct national myths to achieve their own goals, or to

---

25) Ibid.
26) Benedict Anderson, *Imagined Communities: Reflections on the Origin and Spread of Nationalism* (Verso Books, 2006).
27) Thomas J Christensen, *Useful Adversaries: Grand Strategy, Domestic Mobilization, and Sino-American Conflict, 1947-1958* (Princeton University Press, 1996).

justify their actions.[28] He distinguishes three types of national myths: (1) self-glorifying myths, which incorporate claims of special national virtues and false claims of victimization; (2) self-whitewashing myths, which deny past wrongdoing against others states and nations; and (3) other-maligning myths, which describe other nations as evil or inferior.

The most effective way of popularizing national myths is to incorporate them in the process of mass education, particularly into history textbooks and mass media reports. Furthermore, such places as history museums and monuments, as well as, commemorative rituals and celebrations can symbolize national myths and strengthen their position in national memory.

However, national mythmaking theory does not state that ruling elites create a false alternative history. It suggests that when constructing national myths, elite actors "operate within the limits of imaginable possibilities",[29] hence national myths has to contain actual historical facts. Mythologizers, to create myth favourable for their option, use such tools as oversimplifications of facts, and omission of sources and materials that does not support their version of events. For example, it is undeni-

---

28) Other examples of victimhood myths can be found in many works on nationalism. Examples include Omer Bartov, "Defining Enemies, Making Victims: Germans, Jews, and the Holocaust," *The American Historical Review* 103, no. 3 (1998). Ruth Linn and Ilan Gur-Ze'ev, "Holocaust as Metaphor: Arab and Israeli Use of the Same Symbol," *Metaphor and Symbol* 11, no. 3 (1996).

29) Emile Durkheim, *The Elementary Forms of Religious Life , Trans. By Karen Fields* (New York: The Free Press, [1912] 1995).

able that Korea and Poland suffered because of foreign aggression but using victimhood to depict entire modern history and depreciating period of peaceful, amicable relations with neighbouring nations, as well as, forgetting about its own wrongdoing toward its neighbours is a national myth. Mythmaking is a historical process because it is "subjective, one-sided, egregiously incomplete."[30]

Mythologizers often cover national myths with patriotic rhetoric, convincing that nationalism and hostility toward other states lies in the national interest. Those ideas seem to be appealing because public opinion does not perceive them in terms of tools of elite manipulation but as a proof of patriotic thought present in society. The popularity of national myths seemingly associated with patriotism makes relation between former enemy states very difficult. The common acceptance of national mythmaking often causes deepening historical dispute between the post conflict states. In other words, such divergent national myths that whitewash and glorify own country and blame other countries for various past wrongdoings can only deepen mutual resentment and memory gap.

Two main schools of thought in international relations, realism and liberalism, do not perceive human emotions as an important factor in shaping interstate relationships. On the other hand, constructivist thinkers emphasize that many violent

30) Retrieved from Memorial worlds: https://memorialworlds.com/what-is-collective-memory/ (*Word Press* 2012).

conflicts were triggered by human emotions. For the needs of the national mythmaking theory, this study adopts Petersen's notion "that emotion can be a powerful casual mechanism compelling certain political behaviour".[31]

Divergence of historical perceptions between former enemy countries caused by widespread national myths may generate certain antipathy and mistrust in both societies. The victim nation will develop profound grievance toward former enemy. At the same time, due to other-maligning myths, the victim nation will begin to cultivate a feeling of contempt for the former oppressor, especially if there was no clear apology and compensation from its side. In case of former perpetrator country, indulged in self-whitewashing and self-glorifying myths will have no sympathy and understanding for the victim side. Moreover, with time the people of such a country will start to feel aversion toward those who constantly remind of their shameful past. Instead of revising their own history and wrongdoings of previous generations, they will blame victim's obsession with the exaggerated past events.[32]

To sum up, human emotions sometimes can become a dangerous tool. Emotions of former victims can lead to deep antipathy toward the perpetrator, which may be perceived by the perpetrator country as a hostile intention or even a premise of a

---

31) Hue-Tam Ho Tai, "Remembered Realms: Pierre Nora and French National Memory," *The American Historical Review* (2007).

32) He, *The Search for Reconciliation. Sino-Japanese and German-Polish Relations since World War II.*

conflict. In the face of such public emotion, both governments will not be able to achieve any kind of policy compromise, not to mention reconciliation.

The other mechanism, which can also affect mutual perception of former enemies is mechanism of intention. When the former perpetrator evades responsibility for its past crimes and refuses to make a proper apology, the victim country may prepare for the re-attack of aggression. Seeing this, the perpetrator country can read it as a sign of hostile intentions. In conclusion, both countries are likely to develop mutual threat perception based on historiographic divergence and prepare military response in case of foreign attack.[33]

Petersen suggests that the mechanisms of emotion and intention can significantly influence foreign policy by manipulating public opinion and as a result changing the state's foreign policy agenda.[34] He also sets two main corollaries of the two mechanisms regarding different reactions of the public as well as elites. First of all, negative emotions and intentions present in societies of both countries will deteriorate mutual opinion regarding each country. Secondly, negative public opinion will influence the government not to cooperate on specific bilateral issues. Both countries should stop creating and wide spreading harmful national myths to facilitate reconciliation.

---

33) Ibid.

34) Roger D Petersen, *Understanding Ethnic Violence: Fear, Hatred, and Resentment in Twentieth-Century Eastern Europe* (Cambridge University Press, 2002).

In contrast to realist approach, national mythmaking theory makes only one general prediction regarding post conflict interstate reconciliation. "The more divergent two countries' historical narratives after their past traumatic conflict, the more difficult they will be to reconcile; the more convergent their narratives, the more easily the will reconcile".[35] In other words, contradictory interpretations of historical events fuelled by national myths may only deepen the memory divergence between former enemies resulting in permanent lack of reconciliation. When former enemy countries decide to undertake bilateral joint history research, they are very likely to enter the path of deep reconciliation.

III. Reconciliation after World War II

1. Reconciliation between Poland and Germany after World War II

Poles and Germans were not always antagonistic nations. As the "neighbours for a thousand years" for long periods in the history, the two nations lived together in peace. The peace persisted until modern nationalism disturbed the Polish-German relations for a longer time. After Germany attacked Poland in

35) He, *The Search for Reconciliation. Sino-Japanese and German-Polish Relations since World War II.*

1939 - when the terrible crimes were committed by the Germans on the Polish nation through later expulsion of millions of Germans from their homelands in the east in the years 1944-1947, the gap between the two nations has become so deep that a return to normality seemed almost unimaginable.[36]

It took a lot of time before the Germans and Poles made effort to find a common language again. An important voice, interrupting the prevailing silence between the two nations, was the message of reconciliation of the Polish bishops, written at the end of the Second Vatican Council in November 1965 in Rome and the response of the German bishops in December of the same year.[37] In the following decades the dialogue between the two countries began mostly within religious, scientific and literary areas. Gradually, the dialogue between the neighbours began to affect political issues as well. The breakthrough came in the years 1980 to 1981, when the news about Poland appeared in every German household due to media coverage from the Gdansk Shipyard - then still the Lenin Shipyard,[38] where the Polish independence movement began. Increasing number of German citizens became aware that in Poland there was a struggle for freedom and human rights.

The following sections, starting from the dialogue at the level

36) Harry K Rosenthal, *German and Pole: National Conflict and Modern Myth* (University Press of Florida, 1976).
37) Lynn Davies, *Education and Conflict: Complexity and Chaos* (Routledge, 2003).
38) Since 1967 till 1989 known as a Vladimir Lenin Shipyard in Gdańsk

of the churches, present the beginning of the Polish-German reconciliation. The next part describes the difficult rapprochement between Polish and German politicians since the seventies. Last part briefly presents vast field of education and history, as the Polish-German reconciliation also has a cultural dimension. Finally, I make an attempt to draw up a summary, which also includes recent disputes and problems.

Letter of Reconciliation of the Polish Bishops to the German Bishops was an attempt to resume the dialogue. Conciliatory gesture of Polish bishops won the recognition of many well-known figures in the world, while in Poland itself, this matter looked quite different. Poles - who were effectively 'protected' by the censorship from information that the government considered undesirable - knew nothing about the bishops' letter. Only after some time, the letter was published in the little-known, low input weekly magazine "Forum" without a few parts deleted by the censors. Publication of the letter unleashed a real storm. Protests organized by communistic party took place in almost every bigger city. In response to written in the letter words "we forgive and ask for forgiveness" Polish communist authorities opposed the slogan "we will never forgive". The propaganda campaign found a fertile ground, because relations between Poland and West Germany had been disastrous. They did not maintain diplomatic relations.[39)]

---

39) Richard P Sander, "The Contribution of Post-World War Ii Schools in Poland in Forging a Negative Image of the Germans," *East European*

German bishops, responding to this message on December 5, 1965 to this letter could not, in the same sense as the Polish bishops to speak "in the name of Germany". They spoke as representatives of German Catholics, but they could not ignore valid voice of those Germans, who were expelled from various Eastern territories. Integration of more than eleven million in a small area of post-war Germany was a challenging process. The failure of this mission could result in a powerful explosive charge, so the response of German bishops seemed more restrained than the message of Polish bishops. German bishops rejected the recriminations and gratefully accepted the invitation to the celebrations of Poland's Christianity Millennium in 1966, and they repaid with the invitation for the Day of German Catholics in Essen, in 1968.[40]

In July of the following year at the 81 Congress of German Catholics in Bamberg, the German clerics invited a group of Polish Catholics. With time presence and speeches delivered by Polish participants during church ceremonies in Germany has become a matter of course. In 1978, Germany warmly welcomed Archbishop Stefan Wyszynski (1901-1981) and Cardinal Karol Wojtyla (1920-2005), accompanied by a delegation of Polish bishops, in the Fall General Meeting of the Conference of German Bishops in Fulda. After the celebration in Fulda, the whole group visited Cologne, Munich and Mainz (a few weeks later, Karol

---

Quarterly 29, no. 2 (1995).

40) Ibid.

Wojtyla was elected pope in Rome).[41]

It is also worth mentioning the numerous initiatives of the German clergy from early fifties, aimed to promote the mutual understanding and reconciliation with Poland. A particularly important role was played by two organizations: "Action Reconciliation" founded in 1953 by young Protestants, and the Catholic peace movement Pax Christi. Also, the Memorandum of Tübingen written by eight prominent German Protestant academics and scientists published in 1962; and the Memorandum of the Council of the Evangelical Church in Germany (1965) on the Situation of Expelled played an important role in the process. In in later document, for the first time, despite fierce internal disputes, the problem of the Oder-Neisse line was discussed. This discussion was continued in Memorandum Bensberger Kreis (1968). Finally, it is necessary to mention the activities of the Maximilian-Kolbe-Werk association, which in the seventies began to help former Polish prisoners of concentration camps.[42]

Even though, all these initiatives have contributed to mutual understanding between Poles and Germans, both nations could not immediately resolve the political and international legal issues, above all, the issue of the Polish-German boundary. At the end of 1970, Cardinal Wyszynski, in a tone full of reproach,

---

41) Yasemin Nuhoglu Soysal, "Identity and Transnationalization in German School Textbooks," *Bulletin of Concerned Asian Scholars* 30, no. 2 (1998).

42) Sander, "The Contribution of Post-World War Ii Schools in Poland in Forging a Negative Image of the Germans."

wrote to Cardinal Döpfner: "Our so cordially extended hand is not accepted without reservation." Döpfner said in his response: "Surely you are right, that the letter [i.e. letter of the German bishops] seems to be more restrained and written with reserve than your letter [···] but, especially with respect to the Oder-Neisse line issue, we could not have written it differently."[43]

1939-1945 is undoubtedly the most difficult period in Polish-German relations, given the Nazi ideology. As a result of the aggression of the Third Reich, approximately six million of Polish citizens perished during World War II (including 3 million of Polish Jews), several million were displaced, 2 million were deported to Germany for forced labour, and every third Polish university employee, every fourth priest, and every fifth teacher was killed.[44]

In 1945, few people believed that any dialogue between Poland and Germany may still be possible, and the gap created during the war seemed to be impossible to overcome for the next several decades. The conflict was further deepened by the expulsion of German population, which the Allied Control Council accepted during the Potsdam Conference in 1945. Before 1950, more than 3 million German citizens left Poland, and in the seventies, another million -mainly from Silesia and Warmia

43) Wanda Jarząbek, "The Authorities of the Polish People's Republic and the Problem of Reparations and Compensation from the Federal Republic of Germany 1953–1989," *The Polish Foreign Affairs Digest*, no. 4 (17) (2005).

44) Ibid.

regions - left the country.[45] As a result, this problem and the border issue has become a major subject of disputes between Poland and Germany. Even the East German communists, even though the ideology forced them to recognize the new border, tried to oppose, especially in periods of social fermentation in Poland as illegal opposition was becoming stronger.

The same mood was present in West Germany, and the statement of Chancellor Konrad Adenauer (1953) is an evidence of it. In his statement, Adenauer stated that: "No German government will ever be able to recognize the Oder–Neisse Line". It was often used in the Polish People's Republic, especially in the context of the following changes in Polish-German relations after the signing of the Treaty of Zgorzelec. The agreement was signed under Soviet pressure by the Polish prime minister Józef Cyrankiewicz and Otto Grotewohl, the prime minister in the temporary government of the German Democratic Republic. It recognized the Oder-Neisse line introduced by the Potsdam Agreement (1945)[46] as the border between Poland and East Germany. The importance of this treaty was weakened by the fact that it was signed only by East Germany.

Tangible changes in Polish-German relations came with the end of Gomulka's government, on December 7, 1970; Chancel-

---

45) Davies, *Education and Conflict: Complexity and Chaos*.

46) Compilation of the most important provisions of the Potsdam Agreement available on PBS website [http://www.pbs.org/wgbh/americanexperience/features/primary-resources/truman-potsdam/]. Retrieved 8 June 2016.

lor of the Federal Republic of Germany Willy Brandt and Polish Prime Minister Józef Cyrankiewicz signed a historic agreement in Warsaw for the normalization of mutual relations. In this document, the two sides agreed that the borderline drawn during the Potsdam Conference "is the western border of the People's Republic of Poland".[47] What is more, both sides confirmed the inviolability of existing borders, then and in the future and declared that they have no territorial claims. Besides the agreement, another seminal moment took place during Brandt's visit. The famous Warschauer Kniefall, in which Brandt spontaneously knelt in pensive apology in front of Warsaw's Monument to the Ghetto Heroes has become a symbol of the new beginning in Polish-German relations.[48]

Also, in 1970, Gomulka as First Secretary of the Polish United Workers' Party was replaced by Edward Gierek, who supported warming of relations between the two countries. The crowning achievement of his activities was a joint declaration (1976) on the development of relations between the Polish People's Republic and the Federal Republic of Germany, and the agreement on cultural cooperation, the 5-year agreement on economic cooperation and several other agreements.

The next chapter in the history of Polish-German relations was opened in 1989 after selecting the first non-communist gov-

---

47) Władysław Wszebór Kulski, *Germany and Poland: From War to Peaceful Relations* (Syracuse, NY: Syracuse University Press, 1976).

48) Ibid.

ernment led by Tadeusz Mazowiecki. On November 12, 1989, German Chancellor Helmut Kohl participated in the "Mass of Reconciliation" in Krzyzowa, where both politicians passed the sign of peace, a symbol of Polish-German reconciliation.[49] The 'Krzyzowa effect' led to a significant acceleration of the process of reconciliation. A year later, Poland and united Germany signed an official border treaty concerning recognition of the Oder-Neisse line that confirmed all the arrangements of the Treaty of Zgorzelec (1950).[50]

Then, Polish Prime Minister Jan Krzysztof Bielecki, and German Chancellor Helmut Kohl signed the Treaty of Good Neighbourship and Friendly Cooperation in 1991. It confirmed and complemented the earlier agreement and regulated the relations of the Germany and Poland, according to the principles of sustainable peace and security and good-neighbourly cooperation. From the historical point of view, such legal regulation between the two countries was phenomenal; especially that it stated preservation and consolidation of peace, and the compliance with the international law, in particular the Charter of the UN and fulfilment of obligations toward national minorities.

Another important element of reconciliation process included in the treaty concerned intensification and development of cul-

---

49) Sander, "The Contribution of Post-World War Ii Schools in Poland in Forging a Negative Image of the Germans."
50) Jarząbek, "The Authorities of the Polish People's Republic and the Problem of Reparations and Compensation from the Federal Republic of Germany 1953–1989."

tural cooperation and exchange between Polish and German youth. What is interesting, some points of the agreement went far beyond the political sphere - they even included the cooperation in the field of health care. According to the art 34 of the treaty, both countries agreed on a comprehensive cooperation in the field of prevention and protection against infectious diseases and other diseases, such as cancer and AIDS. Germany also expressed strong support for Polish aspirations for integration into the structures of Western Europe.[51]

The treaty was supplemented by three additional agreements in 1992: Agreement on the Polish-German Youth Cooperation, Agreement to establish a Polish-German Environmental Council, and Agreement to establish a Polish-German Intergovernmental Commission for Regional and Cross-Border Cooperation. Such agreements facilitated formation of the Foundation for Polish-German Reconciliation, supporting the victims of the Third Reich and of the Nazi repression and facilitating Polish-German dialogue. The Foundation is also engaged in the issue of payments for former concentration camp prisoners, slave- and forced labour. An important supplement to the real rapprochement was the visit of the President of Germany Roman Herzog in Poland, during the ceremony commemorating the 50th anniversary of the Warsaw Uprising (1994). During this visit the president asked for forgiveness all the Polish victims of

51) Davies, *Education and Conflict: Complexity and Chaos*.

the war triggered by Germany.

The countries undertook several different supra-regional initiatives, which served and still serve not only them, but also provide a model of successful rapprochement policy for rest of the Europe. Those initiatives include Weimar Triangle, an organization founded in 1991 by the foreign ministers of France, Germany, and Poland, in order to develop cooperation between those countries, as well as to assist Poland's emergence from Communist rule. Regional and cultural projects including youth exchange were implemented within the tripartite format. The purpose of such exchange was to overcome the division of Europe and introduce young democracies of Eastern Central Europe countries, mostly Poland, to the community of European countries, and thus to continue the work of building a strong and unified Europe. Once this goal has been realized along with the Polish accession to NATO and the EU, the redefinition of the tasks of Weimar cooperation has become a necessity. In the enlarged EU, Weimar Triangle serves as a forum for consultation and development of common positions on key issues regarding European policy.[52]

The idea of Polish-German cooperation includes also existing on the Polish western border Euro-regions Neisse (since 1991), Spree-Neisse-Bober (since 1993), Pro Europa Viadrina (since 1995)

---

52) Ryszard Zięba, *Główne Kierunki Polityki Zagranicznej Polski Po Zimnej Wojnie* (Wydawnictwa Akademickie i Profesjonalne, 2010).

and Pomerania (since 1995).[53] The activities within the framework of these Euro-regions mainly include environmental cooperation, promoting economic prosperity, cultural development, and the continuous improvement of living conditions of the inhabitants of the regions.

In the Euro-region Pomerania Polish and German uniformed services: police, customs officers, border guards, firefighters, prosecutors, and judges work together on a daily basis. Also, government administrations, employment agencies, and labour unions on both sides of the border cooperate with each other under certain conditions. The cooperation also involves the exchange of information on trends in migratory movements, transports of high-value goods (such as alcohol, cigarettes, and electronic equipment) as well as weapons, ammunition and explosives.

In contrast to the difficult political reconciliation between Poland and Germany, cultural dialogue in the post-war period between the two nations began spontaneously, especially in terms of youth exchange and cooperation. Both governments still attach great importance to cooperation in the field of education. Thanks to the Foundation for Polish-German Reconciliation, young generation has chance to learn and participate in the reconciliation process. It is also worth mentioning that the main motto that guided the Foundation is "Reconciliation

---

53) Jarząbek, "The Authorities of the Polish People's Republic and the Problem of Reparations and Compensation from the Federal Republic of Germany 1953–1989."

through the exchange of youth". The activities the organization are financed jointly by the Polish and German governments, and in November 2013 for the first time in history, support for the organization was written in the coalition agreement of the newly elected government of Angela Merkel.[54]

The rhetoric of reconciliation was successfully implemented in terms of commemoration, which was very important in Polish-German relations. The framework of the cooperation by the two countries brought many educational institutions to life. Some of them, as in the case of cross-border initiatives did not survive but many others are still active and undertake actions aimed at implementation of effective rapprochement policies, like for example: established in 1990 after the meeting of Kohl and Mazowiecki - the Krzyzowa Foundation for Mutual Understanding in Europe. The primary objectives of the foundation are to promote tolerance and heritage of "anti-Nazi opposition". Within the framework of the Foundation, the International Youth Meeting Centre and Memorial in Krzyzowa, were established to cultivate the memory of the movements of resistance against totalitarian regimes.[55]

Another important education institution is International Youth Meeting Centre in Oswiecim founded by the Berlin Action Reconciliation Service for Peace and the Municipality of

54) Zięba, *Główne Kierunki Polityki Zagranicznej Polski Po Zimnej Wojnie.*
55) Michael Cunningham, "Saying Sorry: The Politics of Apology," *The Political Quarterly* 70, no. 3 (1999).

Oswiecim. Its main task is to conduct educational and cultural activities based on the history of the concentration camp Auschwitz-Birkenau for youth and adults from around the world, especially for German and Polish youth. In 2005, the International Centre for Education about Auschwitz and the Holocaust was brought to life within framework of the Auschwitz-Birkenau Museum to disseminate information about the tragic history. Initiatives taken there are addressed to all concerned, and the activities of the Centre go far beyond the program of reconciliation between Poles and Germans.[56]

In contrast, activities of Polish-German European Youth Centre are addressed only to the Poles and Germans, and their activities are mainly focused on youth initiatives. As part of its work, the centre also organizes the so-called stays, within which implements projects to integrate and introduce easy way to better know the past of the two countries and the culture of nations. Through the establishment of so many initiatives at the institutional level, the project of the reconciliation can be implemented not only in the political dimension but also social as well as educational dimensions. It is worth mentioning that above mentioned initiatives, beside ideological support, also received large financial support from the governments of both countries, but certainly the German side has invested incomparably more.

---

56) Zięba, *Główne Kierunki Polityki Zagranicznej Polski Po Zimnej Wojnie.*

Other aspects of cultural cooperation between Poland and Germany are related mainly to art. Cooperation in this respect, despite the lack of political dialogue, has developed rapidly since the end of the War. The Polish Festival of Contemporary Music Warsaw Autumn, even at a time when Europe was still divided, attracted many Western composers and performers. On the occasion of this festival, opera groups and orchestras from Germany toured several times in Poland. Polish orchestras also crossed the border and played in Germany long before the two countries established diplomatic relations.

Polish literature also quickly gained popularity in post-war Germany. Interest in Polish literature existed before, especially when it comes to the classics, such as Adam Mickiewicz, Henryk Sienkiewicz, Wladyslaw Reymont; Polish writers, however, remained in the shadow of Russian authors, who that time enjoyed great popularity in Western Europe. This has changed in recent decades: Polish statistics showed at the end of the seventies, Germany (and German-speaking countries) made the biggest number of translations from Polish, more than in all other countries of the world ("Literature", June 1977). What is interesting, some works of Polish post-war author Witold Gombrowicz have been published first in German, and only few years later in Poland. In other words, Polish literature is present in the circle of the German language in the extent to which it is not present in any other language.

Reconciliation in the context of Polish-German relations appears regularly since the end of World War II. Reconciliation initially considered as a taboo, later present in numerous historical gestures and signs, after 1989 transformed into a specific program implemented by the governments at various levels. The past in the relations between them did not hinder the adoption and implementation of many economic, social and cultural initiatives.

2. Reconciliation between Korea and Japan after World War II

The real efforts to normalize Korea-Japan diplomatic relations started only after Korean President Rhee Syngman[57] left the political scene in 1960. Normalization of the diplomatic relations was mainly caused by the authoritarian Park Chunghee government's need for financial support from Japan to rebuild Korean economy. Although it met with the serious protests of the general public in Korea, the Japan-Korea Treaty on Diplomatic Normalization was signed in 1965. Besides establishing 'normal' diplomatic relations between the two countries, the agreement also provided a legal basis for settlement of claims, as well as more than USD 840 million in economic loans for Korea.[58]

Following Korea's democratization process in the late 1980s,

57) Japanese and Korean names in this chapter are written in the order of family name followed by given name(s).

58) Brad Glosserman and Scott A Snyder, *The Japan–South Korea Identity Clash: East Asian Security and the United States* (Columbia University Press, 2015).

maintenance of relatively normalized political relations has become considerably difficult for both governments. Korean democratic transition has forced Japanese government to convince both the Korean ruling elites and Korean people of the sincerity of its determinations to achieve real reconciliation.

The first real test came in the early 1990s, when the Korean general public was allowed to talk about the issue of so-called 'comfort women'. They were young women from many parts of Asia including Korean Peninsula, forced into sexual slavery by the Imperial Japanese Army in occupied territories before and during World War II. Based on extensive multilevel consultations, the Japanese government decided to acknowledge the suffering of the women and establish a nongovernmental organization the Asian Women's Fund, providing compensation to them and their families.[59]

However, Seoul successfully discouraged Korean victims from accepting the funds claiming that they were provided indirectly by a non-governmental organization, not by the Japanese government. Also, in the 1990s Japanese government issued two statements of apology concerning Japan's colonial past, the 1993 Kono statement (named after Chief Cabinet Secretary Kono Yohei) and 1995 Murayama statement (named after Prime Minister Murayama Tomiichi). The Korean government found them as essential gestures of Japanese will to pursue historical reconciliation.

---

59) Naoko Kumagai, "Forgiveness in Reconciliation Between Japan and South Korea." *E-international Relations* (2016)

A major turning point in Korean-Japanese relations came in 1998 when President Kim Dae Jung and Prime Minister Obuchi Keizo signed the Joint Declaration of a New Korea-Japan Partnership towards the 21 Century. In this declaration, Obuchi expressed "deep remorse" and "heartfelt apology" for Japan's colonial past.[60] The statement was welcomed with appreciation and enthusiasm by the Korean side, which recognized it a solid foundation for further development of "future-oriented relationship." This agreement paved the way for further cultural and popular exchanges as well as expanded political cooperation between the two countries. This change in bilateral relations between them was also welcomed by the US which encouraged the establishment of the Trilateral Coordination and Oversight Group (TCOG) - a high-level coordination mechanism regarding policy toward North Korea.

Despite the positive developments in bilateral relations, since 2000 a series of unfavourable issues obstruct reconciliation process between the two countries. Tensions over unresolved historical issues, such as comfort women and Dokdo/Takeshima Island issue; controversies concerning history textbooks approved by the Japanese government; visits paid by the Japanese prime minister to Yasukuni Shrine, where some class A war criminals are enshrined - periodically emerged inside Korean society

60) John W Garver, *China's Quest: The History of the Foreign Relations of the People's Republic, Revised and Updated* (Oxford University Press, 2015).

obstructing intergovernmental reconciliatory policy. Similarly, cooperation within the TCOG framework lost its priority in the mid-2000s as a result of strengthening of cooperation under the Six Party Talks on North Korea's denuclearization.

With the almost simultaneous elections of President Park Geun-hye and Prime Minister Abe Shinzo in 2012, the relationship deteriorated again. Park during her election campaign emphasized the need for Korea, Japan and China to have a "correct understanding of history to overcome the Asian paradox"[61] of economic growth accompanied by growing security dilemmas. However, the re-election of Abe as Japan's prime minister considered being nationalist and historical revisionist caused a great discontent in the Korean society. Also, US government become more and more frustrated that American rebalancing strategy toward Northeast Asia was being curbed by poor relations between Korea and Japan. Abe's visit to Yasukuni Shrine in 2013 only confirm Korean worries about Abe's revisionism, but at the same time it catalysed US effort to restored relations between its two allies.

In the beginning of 2014, the US made every effort to bring Park and Abe together for trilateral summit meeting on the occasion of the international nuclear security summit in Hague. Korea's initial condition for this meeting was that Abe's public

---

61) Geun-Hye Park, "A Plan for Peace in North Asia. Cooperation among Korea, China and Japan needs a correct understanding of history." *The Wall Street Journal* 2012.

pledge to officially confirm the Kono and Murayama statements. But parallel to this pledge, Japanese Liberal Democratic Party launched an internal reviewing procedure regarding the Kono Statement. This move was perceived by many international observers as an attempt to discredit validity of the statement. However, the Hague trilateral summit proved to be fruitful in terms of facilitating Korea-Japan intergovernmental dialogue. As a result, the two leaders concluded an agreement to hold "director-general-level meetings on how to deal with the issue of comfort women, an issue that Park had previously made the main prerequisite for improved relations.

In the aftermath of Hague summit, Korea and Japan held several cabinet-level meetings. As a result, they concluded the agreement in 2015 establishing the Healing and Reconciliation Foundation with Japanese funds. The agreement that was claimed by the both governments to be "irreversible" has been put into a question by the Moon Jae-in's government that decided to dissolve the Foundation even though 34 of the 47 surviving former comfort women accepted financial aid from the Foundation. According to the Blue House spokesperson "the agreement did not sufficiently reflect the opinions of the former comfort women, and it would not settle the comfort women issue". The Moon government's decision on the Healing and Reconciliation Foundation came in the similar time with a ruling by the Korean Supreme Court that ordered Japanese steel company to pay damages to Korean wartime labourers. That decision has met enormous dissatisfaction from the Japanese side since they agreed to settle issues of compensation in 1965.

Putting the Korea-Japan relationship in the context of reconciliation through forgiveness reveals three problems: perpetrators' unclear acknowledgement of guilt, the victims' sense of engagement in the reconciliation process, and a certain sense of humiliation for both sides. One of the biggest clashes concerns comfort women, and the proper means of objective acknowledgment, apology, and compensation for their traumatic experiences. While the Korean side gives emphasis to the forcible nature of comfort women' suffers and painful experiences at comfort stations, the Japanese side argues that there is no official documentation confirming actual forced character of the recruitment by the wartime Japanese authority. This controversial deduction has opened another discussion over whether the Japanese authorities are legally responsible for harm caused to the victims and own compensation to them.

The intergovernmental agreement reached in 2015 to ultimately resolve the issue of comfort women contains the Japan government's acknowledgement of responsibility and Korea government's acceptance of "Japan's remorse and willingness to cooperate in Japan's efforts to heal the psychological wounds of the victims." However, shortly after the signing of the agreement, Korean comfort women expressed their deep dissatisfaction with the ambiguous provisions concerning the Japan' s responsibility and remorse. Most of the victims also strongly opposed the accord because it was reached without any consultation with them. Even though governments made significant progress in their relations, anger and frustration of war victims continue. The 2015 Korea-Japan agreement, albeit perceived by Western media as "historic", did not bring the forgiveness and did not trigger popular reconciliation.

Genuine reconciliation achieved through forgiveness is very difficult in situations where more than two individuals are involved. Since genuine compassion and atonement are something to feel at the individual level, it is difficult to move it to the collective consciousness. What is clear in the Korea-Japan reconciliation efforts, it the fact that states as political collectivises cannot assume moral and metaphysical guilt. Moreover, the moral and metaphysical guilt same as criminal guilt can be considered regarding the individual who committed the crime, and most importantly can be felt only at the personal level. In this context, the 2015 agreement can be seen simply as a meaningless diplomatic gesture.

The other problem in the process of popular reconciliation is the issue of humiliation concerning both the victim the perpetrator. When former victim forgives, automatically places himself/herself morally above the perpetrator, which may not be important as long as human relationships are concerned but may count at the state-to-state level. Alongside with the decreasing power gap between Korea and Japan since the 1980s accompanied by growing voices for Japan's apologies, a certain resistance against apologies for the wartime atrocities has emerged inside Japanese society.

Genuine people-to-people reconciliation should be pursued in order to complement political reconciliation. While political reconciliation may be changed by different developments in both domestic and international politics, popular reconciliation once attained is hard to undermine easily. In other words, regarding reconciliation approach toward Korea-Japan case, the resolution of history divergence is the key to a significant improvement of relations.

IV. Conclusions

In the different theoretical discourses on interstate reconciliation, there has been much scepticism on the German reconciliation strategy as a model. Some point out the mythical fabricated nature of post-war reconciliation in Europe, and others focus on still unresolved issues in the German national historiography, for instance, approach to the Nazis in unified Germany. All these researches reflect the deepening in perception of historical reconciliation as a constantly changing, open-end process rather than a result-oriented, fixed process.

However, many social and political scientists from Korea and Japan have strived to learn lessons not only from the overall Polish-German reconciliation process but specifically from the experience of reconciling historical narratives. As the knowledge about Polish-German experiences advanced, the Asian counterparts became aware that application of the same patterns in their case is not an easy task. However, European reconciliation experiences were very useful for Koreans and Japanese in learning about the importance of the historical dialogue as well as popular reconciliation. Furthermore, European examples helped Koreans and Japanese to understand the particular differences that their case holds and think about possible future reconciliation policies.

In comparison to the German-French case, the Polish-reconciliation dialogue holds more similarities to Korean-Japanese activities. Also, more similarities in overall bilateral relations between the two dyads can be found: Border disputes, socio-political imbalance between the two neighbours, and finally democratization process in Poland and Korea, which took place long after World War II. Polish-German case has been perceived as a successful story that showed that historical dialogue - an efficient method for improving interstate and people-to-people relations from hostility to reconciliation.

This effective but not yet completed historical dialogue between Poland Germany was the product of several important ingredients: (1) engagement of multilateral actors: political leaders from both countries, UNESCO, Polish and German civil society, including the academic and religious groups; (2) German government's active support; (3) clear division between the political-diplomatic dialogue; (4) implementation of the Ostpolitik by Prime Minister Brandt in order to move forward the historical reconciliation; and (5) continuous work on improvement of history teaching materials and teaching methods.

Both in the case of Poland-Germany, as well as Korea-Japan, efforts to reconcile historical narratives resulted in important, long-range achievements in the field of history education. Firstly, thanks to this process different historians and educators from those countries had chance to discuss the most controversial historical issues. The scholars, who took part in different projects regarding history dialogue, learned a very important lesson how to accept and understand differences and build the foundation for reconciled thinking. This kind of mutual trust and colleagueship should not be limited only to historians and history teachers but developed among different social groups.

In case of both analysed dyads, it is clear that focusing on result-oriented projects does not bring desired results. Thus, the dialogue should not include only historians and history teachers but also should embrace different social groups in order to give chance to broad public to talk and cooperate on different aspects of reconciliation.

The analysed cases address several significant puzzles in contemporary Northeast Asian and European international relations. For instance, why did Korea and Japan discuss historical issues not right after the war was over but only from the time, when the two countries had established diplomatic relations and developed bilateral economic as well as social exchange? Moreover, around that time the majority of Korean and Japanese populations had no memories or direct experience of the colonial era or war. Secondly, during the War Germany and Japan committed unspeakable atrocities against their neighbours. Why did Germany prove much greater repentance and willingness to compensate than Japan?

Selected Issues in the EU-Korea Relations